YEAR OF PLENTY

YEAR OF PLENTY

A FAMILY'S SEASON OF GRIEF

B.J. HOLLARS

The University of Wisconsin Press

The University of Wisconsin Press
728 State Street, Suite 443
Madison, Wisconsin 53706
uwpress.wisc.edu

Gray's Inn House, 127 Clerkenwell Road
London EC1R 5DB, United Kingdom
eurospanbookstore.com

Printed in the United States of America
This book may be available in a digital edition.

Names: Hollars, B. J., author.
Title: Year of plenty: a family's season of grief / B.J. Hollars.
Description: Madison, Wisconsin: The University of Wisconsin Press, 2024.
Identifiers: LCCN 2023043902 | ISBN 9780299347444 (paperback)
Subjects: LCSH: Hollars, B. J. | Hollars, B. J.—Family. | Authors, American—
    20th century—Biography.
Classification: LCC PS3608.O48456 Z46 2024 | DDC 813/.6 [B]—dc23/
    eng/20231114
LC record available at https://lccn.loc.gov/2023043902

Book epigraph: "Consolation," from *Beautiful Trouble*, published by *Crab
Orchard Review* and Southern Illinois University Press. Copyright © 2004 by
Amy Fleury.

Steve Ball, "Celebration of Life," June 24, 2021, and B.J. Hollars, "Farewell, Fort
Wayne," January 11, 2022, are reprinted as "Final Cancer Treatment Preceded by
a Surprise" and "December 26, 2021" by permission of the *Journal Gazette*, Fort
Wayne, Ind.

For Meredith

What would we make of a life both blighted and blessed?
There was trouble all around and everywhere little mercies.
—Amy Fleury, "Consolation"

CONTENTS

III. After

{ I }

Before

November 4, 2020

I'm standing in a lecture hall twice the size of my house. The room is dark, except for the glow of the PowerPoint slides projected on the screens behind me. Who knows what I'm prattling on about. Some days, even I don't know.

"Any questions?"

Weary behind their masks, the eighteen-year-old students make no attempt to respond.

Atop the teaching station, my phone begins to buzz.

Steve Ball. My father-in-law.

My eyes linger on his name long enough for the moment to grow uncomfortable. And then, the buzzing stops.

I return my attention to the students.

"No questions then?" I ask.

The buzzing begins again.

I can count on one hand the number of times my father-in-law has called me. Each time, it was only to reach his daughter Meredith. When we talk, we talk in person: gathered at the neighborhood coffee shop he owns in Fort Wayne, Indiana, or seated in his home adjacent to his shop. But never like this.

If he'd called once, I might not have worried. But he's now called twice, so I do.

"Excuse me," I tell my students, reaching for the phone. "I think I need to take this."

I answer the phone midway out of the classroom, walking swiftly toward the hall. The students' eyes trail me.

"Hello?"

"Hi," Steve says.

"How's it going?"

"Okay."

He tells me he has news to deliver to his daughter, but he doesn't want to do so until I'm home.

"Are you home now?" he asks.

"No, I'm afraid I'm teaching."

"Well, when will you be home?"

"Five forty-five," I say. "Six forty-five your time."

"Okeydoke," he says. "I'll call back then."

Steve does not disclose the nature of his news; he doesn't have to. While at the rental cabin in August, I'd heard his lung-rattling cough. His gravel-in-a-tin-drum cough. His cough, so persistent, that I couldn't escape it even while bobbing in a kayak a hundred yards from shore.

I'd hoped it wasn't COVID. Hoped it wasn't the other thing, either. Better to blame it on pollen, or ragweed—something a little allergy medication might fix.

Standing in the hallway of the academic building, I peer at a birch bark canoe behind glass. I wonder what would happen if I took that canoe out the building's back door, portaged through the parking lot, and sidestepped down the rocky embankment to the river flowing west. What would happen if I hurled my phone against some distant shoreline? If I did not return home by five forty-five?

I press a hand to the cinder block wall. I find my legs and ask them to move. But the ground beneath me has shifted, and it takes my legs a moment to remember what to do.

One foot in front of the other, I reenter the classroom. The students don't know what to make of me. In the span of a thirty-second phone call, I have changed.

I take my place at the front of the room, trying not to think of my father-in-law nine hours away in Indiana. How he has more than likely turned on the Weather Channel, as is his custom, because the Weather Channel can predict the future.

Cloudy with a chance of . . .

Sunny with a chance of . . .

Even the best predictions are always a matter of chance.

I clear my throat; I try for a smile behind my mask.

"Now then," I say, "where were we?"

November 24, 2020

When Meredith hears her dad say, "Stage four small cell lung cancer," she nods and hangs up the phone. Lifting herself from the blue couch, she excuses herself to the garage.

I sigh. Sometimes you know the news before you even hear it. Yet this is not the news he had disclosed a few weeks prior, following the conclusion of my class. That news had sounded optimistic. Something about "dead cells." Something about the need for another biopsy. Nothing to worry about, he'd promised. We'd believed him.

But on this day, when the second biopsy returns, we no longer have the luxury of not knowing. I'd been eavesdropping from the kitchen. The same kitchen where, five years prior, Meredith received a similar call from her mother. The déjà vu is startling. A time warp that we wish we could warp-speed away from. On that January night, we'd uncorked a bottle of "emergency wine" as we readied ourselves for a battle we knew we couldn't win. Her mother's disease had a name: pancreatic cancer. And a timeline: two weeks from diagnosis to death.

It's Thanksgiving break, and our home thrums with the usual aliveness. In the basement, eight-year-old Henry pounds hard on the video game controller, while six-year-old Ellie roots him on.

I shout down the stairs: "Everything okay down there?"

"Yes!" comes the chorus.

"What are you doing?"

"Killing bad guys!" Ellie calls.

I turn my attention to the bedroom down the hall, where one-year-old Millie sleeps. Peering through the cracked door, I lay eyes upon the one member of our family whose ignorance will spare her the bulk of what comes next. I leave the room as quietly as I've come, my feet avoiding each creak of the floorboards, which by now I know by heart. How is it that I can't even know my body half as well as I know my house?

Outside, Meredith balances atop a stepladder near the front stoop, a strand of Christmas lights dangling between her ungloved fingers. Suddenly it is sweatshirt weather, squash soup weather—damp but dry all at once.

"Any good news?" I ask.

"Not really," she says, untangling the strands like a cat's cradle. Her eyes are the color of oceans.

"What are the kids doing?" she asks, sticking a plastic hook to our home's exterior.

"Killing bad guys."

"I see."

For the next half hour, Meredith positions the strands around the doorframe, up the columns, past the picture window, to the outlet in the garage. I play a supporting role, lifting the lights to keep them from dragging against the ground. I might as well do nothing.

She plugs in the extension cord. Together, we wait for the current.

In the time it takes to say, "I'm sorry," the white lights burst to life. Meredith folds the stepladder and returns it to the garage. The work, now done, gives way to other work.

Inside the house, a baby cries, a bad guy dies, and a husband stands in the doorway beneath the eaves.

"I'm starting to wish we were going home for Thanksgiving," I say.

"Yeah," Meredith says as she walks toward the wails. "Me too."

Following a walk around the block, Ellie presses her hand to her heart to learn that her heart has gone missing.

"Oh no . . . ," she says.

"Oh no, what?" I ask.

"It's gone," she says. She means the heart-shaped locket Meredith had fastened around her neck the previous day. And not just the locket, but Meredith's ring, too—which her mother had given her and which she'd threaded through the locket chain for safekeeping. The locket is replaceable, but the ring is not. The difference is lost on our daughter.

Ellie and I retrace our steps: returning first to the discount store where the locket was last seen. The store is glutted with holiday shoppers who fill their carts with everything unnecessary. We walk with purpose throughout the store, zigzagging past bargain bins, power tools, and the rest of the strange assemblage. This place has everything except the things we need. We press our ears to the carpet, scanning the floor in search of a heart, a ring, or both. Clutching Ellie's clammy hand, I wait in line to speak to the young woman behind the register. I explain the situation, stressing the ring's sentimental value. The young woman remains unmoved; there are customers waiting.

I want to add that my mother-in-law has been dead for five years and that this ring was a gift between mother and daughter.

To explain to the young woman that my own daughter mostly only knows her grandmother by way of this ring.

"Can I get your number?" the young woman asks. "I'll call if anything turns up."

When we confess the loss to Meredith, her anger turns to sadness in half a breath. Ellie cannot understand why her mom is crying. Tears, suddenly, have become so unpredictable.

"Did they cost a lot of money?" Ellie asks.

"Not really," Meredith says, holding Ellie on her lap. "But that ring belonged to Mama's mama."

"Oh," Ellie says. And then: "Ohhhhh . . ."

Over the past month, Meredith has regularly traveled between Fort Wayne. I've tried to keep things afloat on the home front, but there are some things I just can't fix. Some things I just can't find, either.

Meredith takes to social media, posting to the neighborhood association page:

Hi all! My daughter lost a heart-shaped locket and a ring of mine with a flower. They are sentimental to me, so if you are wandering around . . .

The next day, I receive a message from the neighbor at the edge of the block. The one I trade waves with as our dogs lunge toward one another from opposite sides of the street.

Hey, she messages. *I found them.*

In the history of miracles, this one hardly makes the list. No one is newly endowed with sight or sound or firmness. No one rises from the dead. It only qualifies as a miracle if a miracle might be considered some ordinary thing.

I run to my neighbor's front door. I take possession of the plastic bag containing both the locket and the ring.

"I was getting my mail," my neighbor says, pointing to the mailbox. "I just saw them there, lying in the grass."

My mind rewinds to the previous day's dog walk with Ellie. I freeze-frame to the moment when it occurred. Her hop-step must've weakened the link in the chain. It was not her fault. All chains grow weak in time.

"Thank you," I say. "You have no idea."

If the woman wonders what makes these items "sentimental," she is too polite to ask. She lost her husband a few years before. She knows that "sentimental" is just another word for "gone."

December 24, 2020

In a different year, we'd scrape the snow from our van, then drive the ice-slick streets toward the church. The defroster would work, or it wouldn't. We'd sing Christmas songs, or not. Always, our exhales would hold in the air just ahead of us, adding something like softness to the night.

In a different year, we'd park on a side street near student housing, walk quickly but safely, our arms overflowing with children. Once inside, we'd endure a gauntlet of greetings from the old men in red and green sweaters, their holiday cheer all but overpowering.

And then, as the volunteers readied the candles for the candlelight mass, all the children in the church would somehow shake free from their parents. They'd gather in pockets of shadows just beyond the sanctuary's high arches. For two minutes, they'd make predictions of the presents they believed themselves destined to receive—whispering the names of those gifts.

We, parents, would then gather them back into the fold, settling into the side pews to begin the business of not causing a scene. We would cause one, inevitably, but all would forgive the trespass. During the Christmas Eve service, scenes are secretly encouraged, less a trespass than proof, for the old-timers, of continuity.

In a different year, at the end of the service, each hand would hold a three-inch candle encircled by a cardboard guard to catch the wax. We'd listen to the same story we heard the previous year and the one before that. About a baby in a manger. About wise men and frankincense and myrrh.

On Christmas Eve night in 2018, as the pastor went on about that baby in that manger, we miscarried. One moment Meredith was singing along to a hymn in the dark, and the next she'd closed the hymnal. Worked her way down the pew and excused herself toward the bathroom near the fellowship hall. I hushed the children as they watched their mother slip beneath the tall arches. Pressed a finger to my lips to hush them as that pastor prattled on with his tale.

Meredith and I took comfort in reminding ourselves that it was "only" a chemical pregnancy—more of a possibility than a promise, and far short of a pact. Still, we will never forget the plus sign on the pregnancy test fading.

But this year is not that year or any other. It is not about what *did* happen, or *might* happen, but what *does*. Since the pandemic has shuttered the church for the first time in a century, we do not descend into that once tranquil darkness. Instead, I scrape the snow from our van and drive us down the ice-slick streets in search of the best Chinese takeout in town.

Twenty minutes later, our meal's disposable containers litter the dining room table. Such a sumptuous spread: sweet and sour chicken and an abundance of egg rolls now gone. All that remains is a drop or two of hot and sour soup dribbling down the one-year-old's chin. Meanwhile, in the living room near the tree, Henry and Ellie engage in gentle warfare with the remnants of the wrapping paper rolls.

That night, all five of us gather in the living room to binge-watch a karate show. Midway through a roundhouse kick, I glance out the window to see low beams. It's our newspaper delivery man. To avoid a Christmas morning delivery, he delivers the news tonight. How much could possibly change over the course of a couple of hours?

Upon hearing the thunk of the paper on the welcome mat, I make my way toward the door.

"Hey!" I shout. "Excuse me."

He turns. Backlit, he is one scraggly Santa.

I hand him a card with money enclosed and apologize for my delay. I'd had his tip by the door for days, I explain, but we kept missing each other. He thanks me, twice. Cheerily, he shakes the card my way like the tip of a hat. Then, he retreats into his warm and rusted van. As he drives toward the elementary school, the ice-encrusted branches bow low beneath winter's weight, while on the ground, the tundra crunches under his tires.

I wipe up spilled soy sauce. I rinse dishes in the sink. I urge the children to say their prayers before bedding down for the night. Sheets tucked, doors locked.

Someone somewhere lights a candle for a thing they cannot change.

I rise so early on Christmas morning that it might as well be Christmas Eve. I slip from the bed and walk down the hall to survey Santa's damage: a big-girl bike for six-year-old Ellie, and a pile of presents for the rest. This is the moment I cherish: not the tearing into paper but the still life just before. The way the predawn glow of the tree dampens the room, adding depth to its dimensions.

I set the needle to the grooves of Nat King Cole's Christmas album, funneling the music down the hall toward the bedrooms, from which the children emerge one by one. Millie comes first, tottering toward me to lay eyes upon our living room transformed—a wrapped wonderland of gifts stacked half as high as she is.

Ellie's not far behind, bending low beside her sister to explain that this is called Christmas. "Remember Christmas, honey?" she asks. "This is it."

Eight-year-old Henry trails, bypassing the others and positioning himself before the gifts that bear his name.

"Can we start now?" he begs.

Fast-forward forty-five minutes and the children are ebullient and beat. Their gift predictions proved true or did not. Regardless, they are mostly happy, mindful that being anything other than happy on a morning like this would trigger some serious chiding by me.

Meredith flips the Nat King Cole album, then lifts her coffee to her lips.

"Thanks for the antiaging cream," I say, reading the back of the tube. "It's almost like you're trying to tell me something . . ."

"Tell you what?" she asks innocently.

I smile, and crow's feet collect in the corners of my eyes.

"Well, everyone," I say at last. "Who's ready?"

And so begins our one and only holiday tradition—embarking upon the nine-hour, 450-mile drive from Eau Claire, Wisconsin, to Fort Wayne, Indiana. There are grandparents to see. And the children have grown desperate for some connection with them beyond the Wi-Fi.

In the preceding weeks, Meredith and I convinced ourselves that we didn't have a choice. Our lives were on pause, but our lifespans weren't. And so, we drive. From Tomah to Wisconsin Dells, to Madison to Rockford. Chicago. Gary. Warsaw. The various "Welcome to Such and Such City" signs serve as the subtitles for our trip. The highways are empty corridors; the gas stations are staffed by skeleton crews. There is something about this zombie world that appeals to me. Whatever trouble lies ahead we can see from a long way off.

Through three states, we listen to holiday music. Through three states, the older children sing along. Out the window, the fields lay fallow beneath their layers of frost. The starched stalks are as flat as a plane. Though I know that yesterday's harvests help nourish the land, there is nothing beautiful in their aftermath.

That night, we do not settle into our childhood homes. We do not eat prime rib with our families. Instead, we stop by my parents' house for an outdoor hello, shivering on opposite sides of a backyard fire while eating chili from Styrofoam bowls. Atop the patio table are bags of grated cheese and oyster crackers. We caution the children not to reach for either with bare hands.

"It's so good to see you!" my mom says again and again.

Since we cannot come into physical contact, "seeing" is the best we can do.

From my place across the backyard fire, I stare at my father's unshaven face.

"How have you all been?" he asks.

It's the only question people know how to ask anymore, even if no one quite knows how to answer.

Fifteen minutes later, as our fingers numb, we exchange small gifts in the gravel driveway. Momentarily, our happiness is renewed. Like the old days but not. Like some new version of the old days, which we fear might become the foreseeable future.

"It's getting late," my mom says. "You better get going to Steve's."

For over a decade, Meredith and I have divided our time between our parents with court-order precision, clinging to some sense of loyalty to our first families. But these days, time is different. Time has evolved. My parents cede theirs as often as they can.

We buckle the children back into car seats, then drive the final mile to Steve's.

Masked, we enter the house adjacent to his coffee shop—a modest, particle-board-floored two-story that looks and feels unfinished. Steve moved here in 2016, about a year after my mother-in-law died.

He chose the house for its convenience. Walking from its back door to the coffee shop, the Java Bean Café, requires all of twenty steps. Steve splits his time between both buildings, though when we're in town, we spend most of ours in the shop.

"Burglars," I call, announcing our arrival as we enter through Steve's back door. This has long been Steve's line, though he seems to appreciate the homage.

Steve's tall frame towers in the doorway between the kitchen and bedroom. He holds a bowl of freshly peeled grapefruit in his hand.

"Boppy!" the kids call from the kitchen, surging toward him.

"Hi, hi, hi!" says Steve, opening his arms to receive them.

Meredith and I follow, the baby and luggage in tow.

A decade back, this drive had seemed so much easier. No kids, no COVID, no need for sleep. Some nights, we'd drive from our then home in Alabama to Indiana in a single sprint, pulling into our parents' driveways shortly before dawn.

One night around 2:00 a.m., we stopped at a gas station off the highway near Muncie. We didn't realize it was abandoned, though we figured as much when we saw the impossibly low gas prices advertised on the rotting marquee. Knee-high tufts of grass gathered alongside the dry pumps. On the far side of the station, a single bulb on a pole threw light as far as it could.

We had to pee, so we did: our old dog found her mark, then Meredith, then me. It seemed the coldest night in Muncie history. So cold that we'd screamed into the frozen air. Howled at temperatures so low they seemed farcical. Otherworldly. For the last hour of that drive, we dedicated every minute to thawing out.

Suddenly that chill is back and far colder than any predawn Muncie wind.

Steve, now standing before me, is not quite the man I remember. Not the one I saw fishing from the pier last summer. Or the one who'd welcomed us with cups of fresh coffee after that long-ago bone-chilling drive.

Henry and Ellie regale Boppy with their extensive list of newly received Christmas gifts while I busy myself attending to Millie's diaper.

"Hey, Dad," Meredith says, hugging him. "Merry Christmas."

"Merry Christmas."

This is the last time they'll say it.

As we approach the downtown hotel, the automatic doors pull open. The bellhop, all but asleep at his post, stirs suddenly.

"Welcome," he says. "And merry Christmas."

Christmas in a hotel is both the best and worst experience imaginable. It is wonderful for its luxury (its chandeliers outnumber the guests) but terrible because it is not our home. That our surviving parents are all within two miles of this place only adds to the indignity.

"Never thought I'd be staying in a Fort Wayne hotel," I say, peering up at the sprawling stairwell. Nodding, Meredith turns her attention to her phone. The children, meanwhile, have commandeered the bellhop's luggage cart. Henry races his sisters through the plant-filled solarium as the girls hold on for dear life.

Had there been another guest in sight, I'd have told them to knock it off. But the hotel is as empty as the highways. We are the only ones there.

I tap the keycard on the lock, then use my elbow to swing open the door to our room. The front desk attendant has assured me that the room has been scrubbed clean of the previous guests. We have no choice but to trust her.

The older kids leap from bed to bed, while the littler one falls into the chasm between them. No matter, Millie is a professional tumbler by now; taking spills is her specialty. Henry and Ellie tear open a bag of snacks and begin to graze. They turn their attention to the television, flipping through the channels in search of cartoons. Millie fights to keep her eyes open—she likes cartoons, too—but sixteen hours have passed since she first stumbled forth from her bed. Her eyelids meet in the middle. Her chin folds into her pajamas' uppermost snap.

"Okay, I think it's time for Millie to go to bed," Meredith says. "And time for the rest of you to get out of the room for a while so she can fall asleep."

"Bye." Millie yawns, her last gasp of second wind as she ushers us out the door. "Bye-bye!"

The door slams hard behind us. Just like that, we are gone.

Henry, Ellie, and I examine our new surroundings in the hotel hallway.

"Well," Henry asks, "what now?"

"What now?" I ask, stalling as a plan develops. "Why . . . now we must find . . . the Christmas spirit!"

"The what?" Ellie asks.

"Come on!" I say, walking briskly down the hotel stairs. "I know it's around here somewhere!"

We leave the hotel and are battered by the wind. We walk directly into it, our faces burning brighter than Rudolph's nose. The empty streets are the opposite of eerie. It's as if someone has pressed a pause button just for us.

"Are we almost there?" Ellie asks, burrowing her head low into her coat.

"Almost where?" I ask.

"I don't know, wherever the Christmas spirit lives."

"You mean . . . here?"

We turn the corner to find the Christmas spirit illuminated on Fort Wayne's only skyscraper: a colored wreath composed of tens of thousands of lights. Amid a circle of cranberries and holly leaves, the message reads: "Merry Christmas."

I'd come here often as a kid, and later, as an almost-adult.

During my last Christmas at home prior to leaving for college, a buddy and I made the same pilgrimage, wasting time on a winter night by (ironically) searching for the Christmas spirit ourselves.

"If that's not the Christmas spirit," I say, "then I don't know what is."

Henry and Ellie crane their necks to see the wreath in full. Its sheer size awes them into silence. They forget, I think, that their grandfather is dying just up the road.

We continue, walking block after block in a city that was once my home. In one of the brownstones, I learned to foxtrot during sixth-grade cotillion class. In another, I attended a friend's father's funeral. Much of these memories have been wiped clean, though their residue remains. If I could train my mind to squint, I could almost see them.

The hotel's automatic doors greet us upon our return. The bellhop has gone home for the night. The luggage cart is tucked tightly behind the grand stairs.

Because it's not yet certain that Millie's asleep, I lead us toward the empty bar at the back of the lobby. The bartender—a woman in her forties pulled straight from central casting—asks, "What'll it be?"

I order a cream ale and a couple of Sprites, distributing the latter among the kids. We walk our drinks to the far side of the lobby. Surrounded by the solarium's plants, we peer out at the rare car throttling past the hotel's wall of windows.

We lift our glasses.

"To Christmas," I say.

"To Christmas," they say.

We take our solemn sips.

Interview #1
Winter 2022

B.J.: Okay. We're rolling now.

Meredith: Okay. So what exactly do you want me to say?

B.J.: I guess I'm just wondering if it would be helpful for you to share what it was like growing up with your dad.

Meredith: Well . . . my dad liked to go on adventures. On the weekends, he was kind of in charge of us, so he liked to take us on the railroad tracks. We went on lots and lots of walks throughout the city. Bike rides. Lots of bike rides.

B.J.: What were some of your specific adventures?

Meredith: I remember one year when the locusts came out. We walked downtown and collected a whole bag full of those locust shells. Then we took them over to my grandma's house . . . I don't know what we were going to make with them . . . a salve or something? It was gross . . . [*Laughs.*] We always went on bike rides to his aunt's house, his Aunt Gladys's house, and we'd ride maybe three or four miles there and three or four miles back. She had a pool, so we'd go swimming there in the summer.

B.J.: Can you tell me about Sponster the Monster?

Meredith: You already know about Sponster the Monster.

B.J.: I know, but for the record.

Meredith: Well, I would always ask my dad to tell me stories, and so he would always tell me stories about a little girl named Meredith Ann who lived in a house with a red door. And the colors changed all the time. Sometimes the roof was blue, or green, or red. Then I would go on adventures. Sponster was one of my allies. So was Molly the Dog, which was just this random dog we met one time that I was obsessed with or something. So Molly would be on our adventures, too. Sponster the Monster and Molly the Dog would always help me defeat the witch. And then, in his witch voice, my dad would always say, "I'll get you someday!" and I would say, "Well, maybe someday, but not today."

January 27, 2021

On this day, our mostly talentless dog reveals his trick. It occurs by accident. One minute, Millie is a one-woman show, blowing into a harmonica, and the next, she's part of a band.

Either Leo loves a poorly played harmonica, or he hates it. All we know is what we hear: his baying, like some seasoned coonhound, bursting through the house. No matter that he's some mixed-breed rescue, for the moment, he's Pavarotti. Meredith and I descend upon the living room from separate sections of the house, bemused by the scene.

Millie's eyes turn wild with delight. Her chest heaves as she all but hyperventilates into the harmonica holes. Leo's vocal range is its own revelation; that dog works his way down the scales.

I turn toward Meredith, who spurts a happy tear or two from the corners of her eyes.

"Um . . . what the hell is happening here?" I ask.

"I can't—" She laughs. "I just can't—"

We haven't laughed this hard since the last time we laughed this hard, and who knows when that was? We'd previously determined that puppies are funny, and babies are funny, but we hadn't yet experienced their one-two punch firsthand.

"Do we . . . intervene?" I ask, making it sound like a diplomatic crisis.

But Meredith can't hear me over the harmonica and howls anyway.

Eventually, Meredith takes a turn on the harmonica, while Millie and I keep rhythm by drumming on our knees. We are, I realize, just a couple instruments short of a jug band.

Leo never relents; he sings until Meredith's breath runs out. Millie and I laugh until it hurts. Then, I take her tiny hands in mine, and together, we spin and spin and spin.

"Okay, how about this one," Meredith says, preparing her next tune. "Do you know this one, Leo?"

Leo knows all of them. Somewhere beneath his fur resides the complete catalog of every harmonica song since the dawn of harmonicas.

Such a small and silly thing, I know. And yet, such a necessary thing.

Our mellifluous mutt belts out a tune, and somehow, we teeter toward rapture.

February 13, 2021

On Valentine's Day eve, I give Meredith the greatest gift I can: one night, alone, in a hotel on the edge of town.

"No kids?" she asks.

"No kids," I say.

"So I can just . . . sleep?"

"All night," I agree.

She doesn't cry, but almost. All she wants is time. Time to think. Time to breathe. Time to reflect on the time now gone. And most importantly, time to plan for more time.

Because the children and I can't possibly allow her complete freedom, we squat in her hotel room for a couple of hours, gorging on Disney Channel and skin-burning showers before taking a dip in the pool.

We enter through the steam-covered door to find a half-dozen couples enjoying their romantic getaways.

I release the children.

"Cannonball!" Henry hollers.

"Cannonball!" Ellie repeats.

"Cannon . . . all!" Millie tries, bobbing after them in her floaties.

All attempts at romance are thwarted; the couples retreat to their corners of the pool.

———

Later that night, the kids and I camp in the living room while Meredith—we imagine—enjoys an ice cream sundae the size of her head delivered directly to her room.

"But can't we just call her?" Ellie pleads.

"The whole point is to give her time to herself," I explain.

Ellie stares at the ceiling, preparing her rebuttal.

"But what if we call just to say good night?"

I turn toward Henry, half-buried in blankets, his face lit up by a screen.

"What do you think?"

"I think that's fine," he says.

Meredith picks up on the first ring.

"How's your big night away?" I ask.

"Fine. Just hanging out at Target."

"Target, huh?"

"Yup."

"Living it up."

"Did you get Millie to sleep?"

"Like an hour ago."

"Wow!"

"Don't sound so surprised."

"I'm just . . . glad."

"It was easy," I lie.

"Maybe she doesn't need me anymore."

"It wasn't that easy," I confess.

If I know my wife, she is steering her cart between aisles with no real direction in mind. She's eyeing price tags on items she doesn't want with leisurely disinterest. Maybe she opens the door in the frozen food aisle to take a breath of chilled air. Maybe she buys one thing—some wholly unnecessary thing—just to tap into the pleasure of indulgence. We are all deserving of a little extravagance now and again, even if we don't believe it ourselves.

"Anyway, we just wanted to say good night," I say. "Everyone say good night."

"Good night!" they call.

"Good night," she says.

The night is neither good nor bad. Meredith and I know a bad night when we see one.

Bear Country
January–February 2015

One late afternoon while preparing for class I receive a text from Meredith: *Bad news.*

We've been awaiting Caryl's test results for days, and though my mother-in-law has already beaten cancer twice, we fear the odds might be against her on a third bout.

I put down my pen and pick up the phone.

"What'd the doctors say?" I ask.

"That there are tumors all over her body."

"Like . . . benign?"

"No. Not like benign."

"What should we do?"

"You should go to class," she says. "You have to teach."

"Yes, but—"

"We can talk about this later."

———

Hours later, I walk home in the cold in the dark—up a hill, across a bridge, and finally, onto a snowy street. I pass the elementary school, the outdoor ice-skating rink, then enter through the storm door and slip inside our home.

I walk down the long hall—bypassing the old dog and infant Ellie, until arriving at three-year-old Henry asleep in his room. As my eyes adjust to the new darkness, I notice Meredith's silhouette alongside him.

"Oh hey," I whisper. "I didn't see you there. Would you rather talk or sleep?"

We meet at the kitchen table moments later. I uncork the bottle of emergency wine. On a different night, this might've been a celebration. But on this night, I can barely even aim the wine within the glasses' wide rims.

Our conversation toggles between stunned silence, logistics, and dread. I steady the base of my glass with both hands. Meredith's left hand hangs low beneath the table, awaiting the old dog's fur.

———

On Valentine's Day 2015, Meredith wakes to a call from her father.

"You'd better start driving," Steve says, "if you want to say goodbye."

Later, I'll learn the facts surrounding that phone call. How throughout the night, Caryl had repeatedly tried to pull herself up from the bed, her anxiety increasing every hour. Fearful she might inadvertently hurt herself amid her nighttime roaming, Steve slept with his feet propped on the edge of her bed. His way of ensuring that he'd wake if she did.

There is a name for it—terminal restlessness—but none of us knew that then.

All we knew was what the nurse had told Steve: that it was only a matter of time.

Over the past two weeks, Meredith had driven back and forth and back and forth again. On this morning, she fills up the gas tank again.

Meredith and ten-month-old Ellie make up the first wave, while Henry and I stay behind. I distract him with every Berenstain Bears book I can get my hands on, taking refuge in a land of well-kept tree houses and chatty bears. In Bear Country, there is a tidiness to the narratives, an inevitable answer that always awaits us on the final page. No matter the problem (a dentist's visit, a messy room, a nightmare), the Bear family always endures.

Throughout the day, Henry and I take one trip after another down that sunny dirt road deep into Bear Country. At the library, Henry sits rapt on my lap as those Bears survive one plotline after the next. When the books run out, we drive to the record store, where his hands mirror mine as we flip through the dollar bins. Eventually, he settles on a Broadway production of *Peter Pan*, while I choose a Stevie Nicks solo album.

Meredith calls as I walk our records toward the register.

"Hey," I say. "How's it going?"

"Okay," she says. "I guess my mom's been asleep all day. They don't think she's going to wake up again."

I place my hand in Henry's curly hair.

"What are you guys doing?" she asks.

I tell her about Peter Pan, Stevie Nicks, and our adventures deep into Bear Country.

"Sounds pretty cooooooool," she says.

Static intrudes upon the connection.

"Are you still there?" I ask.

"I'm losing you," she says. "It's super windy out here. I love—"

———

Seven hours later, while Henry and I drive home from the grocery store, my phone buzzes.

"She's gone," Meredith says. "It's over. I'll call later."

"Was that Mom?" Henry asks.

"It was," I say, pocketing the phone. "Hey, you ready to help me with the pizza?"

We preheat the oven to 425. We set the table for two.

That night, we do not talk about death. Instead, we devour supreme pizza and peach iced tea. We brush our teeth and change into pajamas. With our bellies full and our bodies warm, we retreat into bed, cocooning the blankets around us while venturing even deeper into Bear Country. Over the next two hours, we watch a marathon's worth of Berenstain Bears TV episodes from a DVD we'd checked out at the library. Most of the episodes are innocuous, though Henry is particularly shaken by Too Tall's successful attempt at peer-pressuring Brother Bear into stealing a watermelon from Farmer Ben's field.

"He shouldn't have done it," Henry says with a sigh.

Life is full of things we shouldn't do, I explain. And full of things we should.

Later, once the TV is muted and Henry's asleep, Meredith recounts the details of her mother's death.

How she, her dad, her older sister, and her younger brother had gathered for dinner around her mother's living room hospital bed. When suddenly—midway through her taco salad—Meredith glanced toward her mother and said: "Mom isn't breathing."

Calls were made, and dishes were placed on the drying rack.

Meanwhile, back in Wisconsin, Henry and I boogied down to *Peter Pan*.

February 20, 2021

I should have said, "I understand."

Instead, I say: "Are you kidding? You want to take our kids on a plane in a pandemic?"

A year into it, and still, we know nothing. Or at least not enough to feel comfortable corralling our still-unvaccinated children onto a crowded plane.

It is always a question of risk. And one not easily measured.

Do we risk the children's safety so that they might spend some time with their grandfather in the place he loved the most? Or do we play it safe, forgo the Florida trip, and lose that time forever?

I walk the dog for hours. I think of Steve reposed on his couch, watching the Weather Channel. I think of him peering over the tops of his glasses at newspaper puzzles. Paging through a paperback. Hitting a handball. Baiting a hook. Adhering to the regimen of his strict daily routine.

I think of him, or I try to. But I am also thinking of myself. Am I prepared to deny my dying father-in-law a few days on the beach with his grandchildren? Or deny his daughter, my wife, the memory of her children and her dad roaming the Floridian shores?

When the dog refuses to walk any farther, I unleash him and reenter the house. The storm door announces our arrival.

Meredith sits on the blue couch, her thousand-yard gaze firmly fixed. I wonder what she sees there.

"They'll double-mask?" I ask.

"Yeah."

I work up a syllogism—*If this, then that, then what?*—but the logic does not hold.

Over the past eleven months, even the answers to easy questions have become unknowable.

I think of my family infected on a plane. And how breath, once the hallmark of life, has now taken on new meaning.

"I mean, the world couldn't be that cruel, right?" I ask.

Meredith ponders this.

"It could be," she says.

March 19–22, 2021

No one billed it as "Steve's Last Trip to Florida." Nobody had to.

The night before they leave, I slip a few paperbacks into the children's backpacks. And then, the following day, I video chat with them on the plane, directing them to the backpack pockets where their presents await.

"Awesome!" Ellie says, flipping through the pages of some book from some series she loves.

"Thanks, Dad," Henry says, reading the back copy on his own.

"Nothing for you, Mil," I tell Millie, lowering my voice to a whisper. "Because you can't read."

She laughs at my glitching face on the screen.

"Well, we're about to take off . . . ," Meredith says.

"Love you guys," I say. "Be safe."

"We will," Meredith promises, adjusting Millie's mask. "Everyone say bye to Dad."

"Bye, Dad!"

Just like that, my family vanishes.

———

I know what I know of the trip because of what Meredith, Henry, and Ellie told me. But there's no making up what I miss, only the uneasy knowledge that I've missed it.

That evening, I do not witness their nighttime arrival at the motel and Millie's first glimpse of the ocean. I miss the kids flipping open their suitcases, retrieving swimsuits, flinging their bodies at the mercy of those thunderous midnight waves. I miss their gleeful screams as they test buoyancy in the icy waters. I observe no teeth-chattering aftermath.

But as Henry tells it, when he wakes at dawn and peers out the window, he spots his grandfather—whom he hasn't seen since Christmas—standing in the receding waves. Fishing pole in hand, Steve casts, waits, reels, repeats—a body pressed tall against infinity.

At the sight of him, Henry wakes the others. Together, with varying lengths of strides, they sprint from the motel room toward the ocean, hollering for their Boppy.

"How's he look?" I ask Meredith during a phone call later that day.

"Okay," she says. "I mean, skinny . . . but . . . okay."

"Okay's okay," I say.

"It's better than bad," she agrees.

———

Henry forgets to reapply sunscreen and pays a terrible price. By midday of the first full day, he's almost more lobster than boy.

"We need to get you a hat," Meredith says. "Like one of those old-man hats."

Steve drives them to the store, where Meredith, Henry, and Ellie fan out in search of a hat. Eventually, Henry discovers a wide-brimmed Tommy Bahama and slips it on his head, transforming from an eight- to an eighty-year-old.

When they rendezvous with Steve, they find him pushing Millie in the cart.

"Where did that come from?" Meredith asks, nodding to the comically large plush cow seated beside Millie.

"I was told she needed it," Steve says, straight-faced.

"Cow!" Millie clarifies. "Mine!"

"And who exactly told you that?" Meredith smiles. "I mean, besides her."

"Oh, I don't know." Steve shrugs, pushing the cart forward. "Somebody who works here, I guess."

———

Back in Wisconsin, I spend the weekend alone untangling a "very serious essay." I take my "very serious essay" very seriously because this, I believe, is what "very serious writers" must do. Or try to do, at least, when they cannot be with the seriously ill people they love or the seriously hurting people who love them.

———

For the last two days of the trip, Henry embraces his wide-brimmed hat, wearing it faithfully throughout the motel grounds during our daily video chat.

"And these are the palm trees," he explains, pointing the phone their way. "And here is the pool. Oh, and this is shuffleboard."

He directs me toward the shuffleboard court, where I see several older men who appear to be wearing hats quite like Henry's.

"You're just one of the guys now, huh?" I ask.

"Yup," he says, half hearing me. "Oh, let me show you the ocean. You won't believe this ocean . . ."

I close my eyes, trying to avoid motion sickness as he bobbles me toward the beach.

"Here it is!"

"That's some ocean," I agree.

Next stop, up the motel stairs to their room, where his sisters watch a show while his mom washes her face.

"Where's Boppy?" I ask, scanning the scene.

"Maybe taking a nap?" Henry says.

"It's morning," I say.

"Yeah," Henry says. "Boppy likes naps."

"Can I talk to Mommy?"

He hands over the phone.

"How's it going?"

"Fine."

"How's your dad?"

"Fine."

"Fine?"

"I mean . . . withdrawn. He's just not feeling very good."

"So not fine?" I clarify.

"Correct," she agrees. "Not fine at all."

March 23, 2021

On the final night, they snap photos beside the ocean.

"Smi-ile," Meredith says. It is worth trying.

No sooner does the photo session end than the kids hurl themselves into the water, fully clothed. They are unstoppable, and what is the point of standing in their way?

Laughter ensues. Splashing ensues. Saltwater, I imagine, coaxes briny tears from their eyes.

"Henry," Steve calls after a time. "Let's take a walk, just you and me."

They walk for half a mile, strolling the beach at dusk as the water recedes from the shore.

"Okay, Henry, here's the game," Steve says, bending down to retrieve a stick. "You take this stick, and you stick it into the sand when the waves go out. Then you have to run away before the waves come back. We're going to see who can get the stick farthest in the water without the water catching us."

Henry's eyes widen. If it's not the greatest game of all time, it's close.

"What's it called?" he asks.

"The Stick Game," Steve says.

They play until the ocean claims every stick on the beach, then turn their attention to the shells with their foiled interiors. Henry holds tight to the shells, loading his pockets even as they weigh him down. He will give them a safe home on a bedside table. Or in a tin can in a drawer among rocks. What he cannot do, he determines, is leave them there unadmired.

Again, I witness none of this. Not the Stick Game or the shell collection or Steve strolling across the lip of the ocean. Not his early-morning fishing, or his midday fishing, or his late-night fishing. Not his early-morning naps, or his midday naps, or his late-night naps. Not the way the tide momentarily throws him off balance, like a great ship keeling. The way he eats or doesn't.

I miss Millie's first marvel at the ocean. And I miss Steve's last.

I should have been there, I realize too late.

In my mind's eye, I see everything: the ebb and flow of water, the young man in the old man's hat. The shuffleboard court and the flock of seagulls gliding past the pool. The crabs with their tiny pinchers. The wet swimsuits on the railing. The half-eaten box of donuts beside the queen-sized beds. The old man hobbling with the old woman's hand in his own. A pile of newly acquired paperbacks. A ball cap with an almost-broken bill. The children tiptoeing past their snoozing Boppy. My wife, peering at the motel fan.

A family, quietly capsizing.

April 16, 2021

My mom rises before dawn to make the long haul to Wisconsin. From Warsaw to Gary, Rockford to Chicago. Wisconsin Dells. Tomah. Eau Claire. All those miles and hours so that she can live her dream of picking up her grandchildren after school.

Together, my mom and I walk from the house to the edge of the playground. With every step, I perform the grown-up-son shamble, walking awkwardly but confidently en route to the school. I have reached an age where I don't quite know what to say to my mother. Anything I say, I fear, may cause her to worry more. Thankfully, she talks enough for us both, remarking on the friendliness of our neighbors, the upkeep of their homes, and the weather, which today telegraphs a once unthinkable spring.

"It's like Mayberry," she says as a pair of young parents steer their bicycles toward the school. "Everything here seems so perfect."

"We like it," I agree. Though we'd like it more if our parents weren't 450 miles away. We arrive at the playground two minutes before the bell.

"So they come from that door?" my mom asks, pointing.

"Usually that door," I say, redirecting her gaze.

She nods, securing the information. "That door," she repeats.

The bell buzzes and the students stream forth. The low rumble of laughter gives way to louder laughter, which gives way to cheerful screams. Backpacks hang heavy atop shoulders much too small for them. Most of the children look like turtles under duress.

I reach for my phone to capture the rare moment. The one where Ellie spots her grandma in the distance and bolts across the soccer field. My mom bolts too; she is the fastest grandma alive. They run, arms outstretched, as if performing a scene from 1940s cinema. Cue the music, ready the close-up: they embrace, their bodies a nearly perfect fit.

They are as happy as meadowed horses. As happy as joy-filled birds in a bath.

"Oh!" my mom cries. "Oh! It's so good to see you in person!"

Ellie flings the monkey mask from her face, then stares at the grandma whom she has not seen—besides on screens—for four months.

I pocket my phone. I capture nothing. Instead, I live a little.

April 18, 2021

For the first fifteen minutes, we don't make it twenty feet from the shoreline.

"What if we try this," I say, pulling Ellie's six-year-old frame closer to me in the kayak. "Now sit tight. Let me do the paddling for a while."

I drape my arms around her to find momentum on this glassy, oxbow lake. Yet so far, momentum eludes us. We are two people with two paddles in one kayak, yet the mechanics don't align. My paddling offsets her paddling, and hers offsets mine. And so, we spin and spin and travel nowhere.

At last, Ellie allows the paddle to go limp in her hands, resigning herself to letting Dad do the work. It is not her preference. For her, self-reliance is a survival tactic—one she's acquired in her role as the middle child.

I dip the paddle off the right side, trying to manage something resembling a rhythm. Due to our sloppy start, the water now puddles in the kayak's crevices. Where our feet should be, and our legs, and our backsides, all we feel is water. Still, we are in good spirits. And wide awake thanks to the morning sun sprawling across the lake's surface.

Seated now with nothing to do, Ellie fits her eyes into my binoculars. She adjusts the focus wheel to spot a pair of Canada geese appearing crisply through the lens. Even at a hundred feet, the birds are bigger than I expect.

They collide with the water with such a stunning lack of grace that I question natural selection. I wonder if they think the same about our kayaking skills.

Ellie turns toward me, whipping my face with her half ton of curls.

"Dad!" she says. "Look!"

"I know!" I say. "I see them!"

For ten seconds, we watch the geese shake the water from their dirt-encrusted feathers. I give chase as inconspicuously as I can, angling the kayak slightly—but not directly—toward them.

I keep my gaze askance as if to say: *Nothing to see here. Just two people in a kayak minding their own business . . .*

But we are not. Instead, we embroil ourselves in their drama.

Stiffening their necks, the geese swim toward the bay's entrance. We follow close behind, gliding into the narrow waterway that widens around the bend. The red-winged blackbirds shriek at full volume—*conk-la-ree*—droning out the sound of our paddling. We are invisible, or so we think, and steady ourselves behind a patch of bramble.

Had we seen the geese from the shoreline, they might not have registered. But joining them on the water feels different. As if we could no longer be observers, even if we wanted.

From overhead, two additional geese clatter into the water. They are as inelegant as their brethren. They greet one another with frantic honking, torpedoing toward their doppelgangers in the water. Ellie and I watch with equal parts fascination and horror. What is the cause of this feather-ruffling?

The males mirror one another, their muscular necks arching like cobras. They circle endlessly, swimming just out of beak's reach.

I feel for the combatants, one of whom will surely lose. What then? Do geese fight to the death?

Suddenly a third pair enters the scene. They join the chorus of honking, floating on the fringes of the watery arena.

"Dad . . . ," Ellie whispers. "What should we do?"

I might've said, "Let nature take its course."

Instead, I scream: "Ahhhhhhhhhh!"

For a moment, even the red-winged blackbirds turn silent, though the geese pay little mind. I scream again, slapping the water with my paddle and trying to make myself big. I fool no one. By now, the geese are so lost in the throes of battle that I'm little more than a backdrop. Not some apex predator, just some middle-aged dad in a kayak on a Sunday morning.

Before this, I was under the impression that nature functioned with some level of predictability. That if observed long enough, the geese might reveal some pattern. If so, their pattern remains elusive to me. All I see is all-absorbing, fully focused warfare.

The honking turns to hissing; we are helpless. And scared. I think again about how they are bigger than I imagined. Big enough to descend upon a kayak if they wanted. And wild enough to strike us with their explosive necks and beaks.

I wonder if we are the cause of the ruckus. Had we drifted too far from the shoreline or paddled too close to the nest? And what are we to make of the second pair of geese? Did they have their own scores to settle? And what of the third pair—the greatest mystery of all? What role could they possibly play beyond voyeurism?

And then, as fast as a stick snapped beneath a boot, it's over. The voyeurs fly off, followed by the second pair, while the first pair reunites beside the reeds just twenty yards away. There are no mortal wounds, no blood in the water, but we are shaken.

I paddle us toward the shoreline near the bay's interior, the kayak's nose parting the lily pads before closing again in our wake.

Suddenly, a couple of college kids emerge from the cattails.

"What the hell was that?" the young man asks.

I tell them I have no idea.

"I mean . . . it was like they were going to kill each other!" the young woman says.

"You're right," I say. "It was nuts."

"They must have a nest," the young man says. "I bet they were protecting some babies. Had to be babies."

I nod. Had to be babies.

What but love might elicit such violence?

Punch Line
March 2014

One night when Meredith is pregnant with Ellie, she asks me for
a glass of water. It's late, and though it is a minor request, I still
grumble as I sleepwalk to the kitchen. Who can say what time
it is? Even the clocks are asleep. But the water is there, and the
glasses are there, so I fill one to the brim. This is no hyperbole; I
literally fill a glass to the brim, measuring each droplet until the
water forms a perfect plane. This is my idea of a joke.

Meredith and I are exhausted, so we work in laughter wherever
we can.

"Here," I say, straight-faced. "I've come bearing water."

"Why do you insist on doing this?" she asks.

(The last time she'd asked for a glass of water, I'd brought her a
pitcher instead.)

"You're welcome," I say as she lifts herself up and chugs. "The
pleasure's mine."

And then, I feel another joke brewing—this one even better
than the first.

I open my mouth but choke on my laughter.

"What?" she asks, placing the glass alongside the fetal Doppler
on the bedside table. "What's so funny?"

I shake my head, hold up a finger.

"What?"

I restart, compose myself by sliding a hand down my face.

"Now that—" I snort. "That there's—"

"That there's what? Seriously, why are you laughing?"

"Now that there's some good . . ."—I pause, waiting for the
punch line—"water."

Maybe you have to be there to get it. Maybe you have to be us.

And maybe you have to know that the part that isn't funny (assuming there's a part here that is) is that I can count on one hand the number of times she's asked anything of me.

My slaphappiness spreads, and soon, she, too, is laughing.

"Quiet," Meredith hisses, nodding toward two-year-old Henry's room. "You'll wake him."

"But that there water . . . ," I say, wiping tears, "that there was some good water, huh?"

"That's not funny," she says, but by now we're laughing so hard she's beginning to wonder if maybe it is.

Maybe this is funny, and maybe our boy's low-grade fever is funny too. Maybe exhaustion is funny, and future-daughter's hiding heartbeat is funny, and every fear we'll ever face is just some form of funny.

"That there—"

"Stop talking!" she repeats. "You're seriously going to wake him."

"Or her." I laugh, pointing to my wife's belly. "Maybe I'll wake her, too!"

The joke stops because now I've made her real. We'd found her heartbeat just an hour before, and I'd grown bold, said a thing when I shouldn't have said a thing.

"Come on," she says. "Just shut up and come to bed."

Actions are easy when you are told just what to do.

May 1, 2021

"Hey, Dad?" Ellie asks as I toss another log onto the backyard fire.

"Yeah?"

"What's your favorite time of day?"

"Mmm . . . probably the morning. Like 6:08."

"Why?"

"Well, because the day is still fresh. I've just woken up, and maybe I've had a cup of coffee, and I'm about to get some writing done. Plus, I know you guys will be waking soon, and then I get to stop writing and hang out with you."

"My favorite time is 6:30," Ellie says, "because I like how it looks on a clock."

"A.m. or p.m.?" I ask, setting my trap.

"Umm . . . both!"

"Correct!" I say, high-fiving. "Because it looks the same on a clock. The hands are the same."

"Yup."

I reach for a stirring stick. The night is dry and warm.

"I used to like 11:11," I say. "All those ones. Plus, people say you're supposed to make a wish at 11:11."

"Oh, then 11:11," Ellie says. "That's my new favorite time."

"But what about 11:04 a.m.? That's a good one too. Maybe you sneak in an early lunch, take a little walk before getting back to work."

"I also like ten—wait, does p.m. mean night?"

"It does."

"Then 10:00 p.m. because I know it's night. It's always dark, and you can tell."

"Hold up . . . what are you doing up at 10:00 p.m.?" I ask.

She blushes.

"Wait, what time is it now?" she asks.

"6:29."

"Then I also like 6:29," she says, nodding toward the west. "I like the way the sun looks this minute."

I turn to watch the yolk break against the clouds.

"You're right," I say. "6:29 is a good minute too."

May 18, 2021

Tuesday, 7:35 a.m., and again, the house thrums with aliveness.

Meredith reaches for her phone, mask, water, and lunch before pausing to take inventory.

"Okay." She sighs. "What am I forgetting?"

"Car keys?" I try.

"Yeah, but I know where those are."

We scan the living room, where the children are hunkered down with books and blocks and screens. We scan the kitchen, where uneaten cereal floats to the tops of their bowls.

"I guess you're all set," I say.

She snaps out of her trance and looks at me apologetically.

"I've got my haircut after school. Did I tell you that?"

"You did, but I forgot."

"Do you have something?"

"Not until seven."

"What's at seven?"

"I'm hosting a book talk. It's virtual though, so I can do it from the basement."

"Okay." She nods. "Good. I should be done way before then. I'll figure out dinner."

I nod, then return her apologetic look.

"After the book talk," I say, "I told Bill I'd maybe go for a walk with him. Just around the block."

"Oh."

"But I don't have to," I say. "We can just see how things go."

"No, it's no big deal," she says. "Millie will be asleep by then."

"We can hope."

Leo scratches my leg, desperate for his own walk.

"What are you teaching today?" I ask, reaching for Leo's leash.

"Myths."

"Do eighth graders like myths?"

"Sometimes," she says. "What about you?"

"I like myths."

She rolls her eyes. "I mean what are you teaching?"

"Just virtual conferences all afternoon."

"How's that going to work?"

"Well, Millie's going to nap. Aren't you, Mil?"

"Yes!" Millie agrees, returning her attention to a book about a snuggly puppy.

"Which means she probably won't sleep tonight," Meredith says.

"Which means probably no quick walk with Bill," I say, completing her line of logic.

We sigh. We can half do our jobs, and half live our lives, but there's no chance we can ever fully do both.

Meredith's eyes fall to the blue couch, where she sat, eight months prior, when her father first said, "Stage four small cell lung cancer."

Nine hours away, an Indiana couch lies empty. Steve will return there in a couple of hours, but first, he's got his coffee shop patrons to attend to.

A moment passes before Meredith's eyes snap back into focus, surveying the living room one last time.

"Okay," she says with a sigh. "Well, I guess that must be everything—"

"Badge!" I say. "Your school badge!"

"Badge!" she agrees. She paws through her purple bag until

retrieving the lanyard upon which it is hooked. She slides the lanyard past her honey-colored hair and around her neck. She smiles as bravely as Athena.

"Love you," she says.

"Love you."

"Love you guys," she calls to the kids.

"Love you!" calls the chorus.

She's out the door, while Leo and I trail close behind.

The dog sniffs the first blooms of the pear tree as Meredith reverses out of the drive.

Interview #2
Winter 2022

B.J.: What else do you remember from your childhood?

Meredith: Well, when I was probably in first or second grade, he moved to Chicago for work. So throughout the week, he lived in this little weird underground apartment in Chicago. Then he'd come home on weekends, and that's why we spent pretty much the entire weekend with him because my mom had us all week. I remember we always took a bike ride on Sundays, and I always kind of felt sad. I had trouble sleeping on Sunday nights because I knew that by the morning, he'd be gone.

B.J.: What kind of work was he doing then?

Meredith: He worked for chemical waste management.

B.J.: That was just a couple of years?

Meredith: No. That was six or seven years.

May 29, 2021

If we'd known that night that he'd be dead in a month, we might've done things differently. Or we might've done things exactly as we did—took a chance, rolled the dice, got a sitter, and sat down, together, in a restaurant, for the first time in fifteen months.

Meredith and I had debated endlessly about the risks. And did everything we could to minimize them. Including arriving at the Cajun restaurant a few minutes before five.

We sit at a high-top table just to the left of the door. Meredith looks beautiful. But we've been married so long that it feels strange to tell her this without turning it into a joke.

"Look at us," I say, as we remove our masks, "freshly showered and without our children."

"We did it," she agrees.

It is no small thing. Most mornings, we can't even use the bathroom without a three-piece marching band parading its way toward the toilet.

"Welcome," the waitress says. "Can I start you two off with something to drink?"

We place our drink orders. When she's out of range, I whisper, "I sort of forget how this works."

"Going to restaurants?"

"Going anywhere."

Behind Meredith's shoulders hangs a framed photo of a high school football team from a bygone era. Sparkly-eyed players who, a century ago, once roamed these downtown streets. Boys barely seventeen who once hitched a horse to a wagon or took a ride in a Ford Model T. Boys who avoided the world wars or didn't. Boys who came home alive or did not.

"They were so young," I say, glimpsing the sepia-toned image. "I wonder if they were any good."

The waitress returns with our drinks, then wipes her hands on her black apron.

"Are we ready to order?"

Gumbo for Meredith and rosemary parmesan chicken for me. We thank the waitress so profusely I suspect it's a little unnerving.

"I guess it's coming back," I say. "How all this works, I mean."

She nods and leans toward her water straw.

Some couples finish each other's sentences, but we don't even start ours. These days, we do most of our talking in shorthand. A look. A sigh. A lift of the left eyebrow. Silence, when properly yielded, can say everything.

I want to laugh, listen, and converse on a topic other than the logistics of our lives. But these days, logistics are our lives. Determining who will drive whom to where and when is as sparkling as our conversations tend to get. It is our great conundrum: how to escape our beautiful kingdom, if only for an hour or two.

Back in our long-distance college days, we'd dedicate most of our Friday nights to phone calls in which we traded questions about our future.

Did we want kids? How many? Boys or girls or both?

Where would we live? What would we do there? Where did we hope to travel?

In all those nights, not once did we broach the subjects of pandemics or cancer—or the potential for both. Back then the future was an endless ribbon unspooling toward infinity. A place we couldn't wait to inhabit filled with people we couldn't wait to meet.

"Well," I say, peering around the nearly empty restaurant. "Should we take a picture?"

"You want to take a picture?"

"To commemorate the occasion," I explain, nodding to the football team. "Like those guys."

She moves to my side of the table, where we do our best impression of a middle-aged married couple struggling to take a selfie. It comes naturally. The first few shots only photograph my finger, but at last, we capture one that accurately reflects our current mood: slightly shell-shocked.

We post it to social media—our lifeline for connection—along with the phrase: "Going . . . out?"

Within seconds, our friends flood the comments section.

For real?

Did you do it?

What's it like out there?

"We're trailblazers," I say, placing my phone face down on the table. "And who knows, maybe we won't even get COVID."

Distracted, she half smiles out the window.

A few blocks away, by the river, throngs of swimsuit-clad twenty-year-olds empty their lungs into their inflatable tubes. Soon, they will place their lives at the mercy of the river, entering upon its placid shores before the current guides their tubes to the boat ramp miles away. Throughout their route, they will sip beers and occasionally lift their eyes to the scenery. They will languish in the waning sun like a burger too long on the grill. No matter. Within a week, they'll shed their skin and start over again. Youth is nothing if not a time to repeat your mistakes.

When we were their age, Meredith and I were too busy plotting our futures to leave much time for mistakes. All those Friday nights on the phone were dedicated to navigating our way around them. Most of those questions, I realize now, boiled down to one:

What would make us happiest?

If we'd known then where the ribbon would lead, would we have followed it still?

The waitress places our steaming food before us.

"Anything else you two need?"

May 29, 2021
(continued)

I lie in the backyard hammock for the first time all spring. Eyes closed, I hear the squeal of the screen door, followed by the pitter-patter of feet.

"Hey, Dad," Henry says, climbing atop the woodpile.

"Hey, bud," I say. "What's up?"

"Nothing much."

"Just wanted to hang out?"

"Yup."

With me? I think.

"That's cool," I say. "How was your day?"

"It was good. Except for the dead snake on the bike trail."

"That was gross," I say.

"*Really* gross," he agrees.

"But our picnic was nice."

"Yeah."

"And you had fun with the babysitter tonight?"

"Uh-huh."

I am desperate to keep the conversation going and scour my mind for any subject that might be of interest to him.

Tell me about Minecraft, tell me about Mario, tell me about Pokémon . . .

What is it he loves this week?

He starts in on a Mario soliloquy, and I do my best to listen. I nod, maintain eye contact, and ask the occasional question.

Half his lifetime ago, Henry and I attempted to spend nearly every summer night on this hammock. The idea of him joining me on a hammock tonight seems impossible.

"You're a good big brother," I say suddenly.

He pauses mid-Mario spiel.

"Why?"

"I don't know why. You just are."

"But why'd you say that?"

"I don't know," I say.

Because it's true, I think.

I see the way he curls up with his sisters on the couch. The way he dilutes their fears with jokes and books and games. And how it's taking a toll on him, too. And how he bears it differently. This is not how it was five years ago when he lost his grandmother, or last year when he lost his dog. He has reached a moment in his life when he can neither defy death nor ignore it. He has reached a moment in his life. And though there will be other moments, the moments he is living now will do much to define him.

I save my speech for another day as Henry eyes the trampoline to our left.

"Shall we jump?" I ask.

Soon we are soaring. The tops of our heads brush the lowermost branches of the trees. The crows retreat to the nearby telephone poles, eyeing us from their too-close range.

Good Dog
March 2020

An hour before her death, I reach for the skillet, then prepare for Cici—our twelve-pound mixed breed—the best fried egg this side of heaven. She scarfs it with such gusto that I offer her my egg too.

Then, the children's eggs.

"But . . . ," five-year-old Ellie protests as I place her plate on the floor.

"Shh," I say, "there will be other eggs."

Endowed with more lives than any cat, Cici specialized in survival. Four years back, when she was diagnosed with diabetes, we figured she had months. The following year, when the vet discovered the tumor, that timeline shrank to weeks.

Three days before she died, Cici sniffed her way to the dryer vent on the far side of the house. She dug a hole and lay down there. She'd never been much of a hole digger, so this took me by surprise. She'd been blind for years—one of the ravages of diabetes—but when she looked up at me with her cataract eyes, her message couldn't have been clearer.

A good dog knows when to stay. A great dog knows when to go.

———

In the six months leading up to Cici's death, I slept beside her on the living room floor. Her bladder had lost some of its lasting power, and rather than force her to endure the indignity of a pee pad, it seemed easier for all involved just to nuzzle me awake. She did, every morning at 4:00 a.m.

During our last backyard roaming, Cici and I sat on the deck steps and peered out into the predawn dark. Seated there, I thought of a long-ago night when we were stuck in Chicago traffic, and how an inconsolable three-month-old Henry had wailed while trapped in his seat. The car was so small, and our bodies were so big, that neither Meredith nor I could wrench ourselves into the back seat to comfort him.

I like to think Cici knew what she was doing as she dragged her body over the console and positioned herself squarely atop our boy. Henry's screams turned to snores within minutes.

———

Grief strikes hardest when you least expect it: the squeal of the screen door, the clink of the food dish, the absence of skittering claws failing to find purchase. A week after her death, muscle memory prompted me to slip a piece of bacon beneath the table, only this time, there was no one there.

Shortly after, when leaving the shower, I was startled to find Cici's name scrawled in the mirror fog.

Is it a sign? I wondered. Some otherworldly message?

It was not, just eight-year-old Henry's way of calling his dog back to him.

Hours after driving home from the vet, my family and I gathered around the table for lunch. At our feet, we discovered one of Cici's heart-shaped dog treats.

Maybe, I thought, she was saving it for later. Or maybe, she was leaving it for us.

May 30, 2021

Following an early-morning dog walk, I enter the house, unleash Leo, and spot the birthday girl, all curls and smiles.

"Well, how's it feel?" I ask.

"Great!"

"The big oh seven."

"Yup!"

"It's Boppy's birthday, too, you know," Meredith calls from the kitchen.

It's the kind of cosmic symmetry that makes everything more manageable. When Steve runs out of birthdays, Ellie's will remain.

———

The rest of the day unfolds in its nearly perfect pattern. By midafternoon, Ellie's friends traipse into our home, masked and ready to party. To the bafflement of everyone, Ellie has selected "mountains" as her theme. Since this theme does not come with any premade cakes, Meredith spends the morning frosting a mountain range atop a cake—three chocolate peaks outlined by a blue icing sky.

The afternoon sun turns to drizzle, complicating the tie-dying portion of the party. Still, the partygoers take their places in the rain, squirting rainbows of colors from plastic bottles into their wadded shirts.

Directly following, Meredith leads the partygoers in a painting activity. On Ellie's orders, everyone must paint their favorite mountain range. At seven, most partygoers have not yet committed to a favorite; there are too many to choose from, they explain.

If it is not the longest three hours of my life, it is close. It is not time's fault. Not the partygoers' fault, either. I am simply out of practice with having so many kids in the house.

At 5:00 p.m., when the parents arrive, I anxiously distribute the party favors.

One for you, one for you, one for you. And don't forget your mountain range painting!

By 5:05, Ellie and I are buckled into the van.

"Thank God that's over," I say. "Now the real fun can begin!"

"But Dad, I had fun . . ."

"The *real* fun," I repeat.

In what is supposed to be a memorable birthday adventure, I pack the life jackets and kayaks and drive us back to Braun's Bay— the sight of the geese's battle royale. I've returned us for the "real fun" so that she might replace a bad memory with a better one.

The weather has other plans. By the time we pull into the gravel lot, the drizzle transforms into something just shy of a torrential downpour. Still, we persevere; I paddle both of us in our single kayak as we return to the narrow inlet. The rain hits the water's surface and bounces back, creating the illusion that it's moving in both directions.

We scan the bottom of the bay for clues of those who came before—some lost toy, perhaps, or an ax blade once belonging to some long-dead lumberjack. Instead, we find a Titleist 3 golf ball, which has become the strange currency of our adventures. Anytime Ellie and I go anywhere, we unearth a golf ball. Almost always a Titleist 3. Over the course of the year, half an egg carton's worth of golf balls has accumulated on Ellie's bedroom shelf.

Ball in hand, Ellie leans back against the front of my life jacket. I revel in a moment that I worry will not come again: such closeness. The plink of the rain on the surface sounds like some lost xylophone key. We close our eyes, listening as the droplets attempt to permeate our skin.

Since we can't outlast the weather, eventually, we return to shore.

"You'll remember this forever though, right?" I ask, dragging the kayak to shore.

"Uh-huh."

"But like . . . in a good way?"

"Sure."

"Not in a murderous geese way, or like a freezing rain way, but just in a 'really fun day with your dad' way"?

"Okay."

Opening the van's trunk, I heave the kayak inside.

"Learn any valuable life lessons out there?" I ask.

"Yes," she says, peeling off her shoes. "Never wear socks in the rain."

———

That night, shortly after kayaking, Steve calls to sing Ellie happy birthday. Moments later, we echo the song back to him.

"How was your birthday?" Meredith asks him.

"It was okay."

"What'd you do?"

"Spent some time with my sister, hung out with the guys at the coffee shop . . . that's pretty much it."

"No cake?"

"Nope."

Seated in our living room, no one quite knows how to fill the silence. I pray for Millie to release some playful baby banter, Henry to prattle on about books, or Ellie to mention the newly discovered golf ball in the lake. Maybe, if I find the harmonica, Leo could howl us a tune.

In a different year, Steve and Ellie might've blown out the candles together. We'd have ended the night with a walk around the block with the dog.

"Okeydoke," Steve says. "Talk to you guys later."

I imagine him as I always do—seated on the couch, peeling a grapefruit, watching the Weather Channel.

That night, I fall asleep on my own couch, waking a few minutes before midnight to see Ellie's number 7 helium balloon drifting ghostlike down the hall.

Premonition (n.): a strong feeling that something unpleasant is about to occur.

June 1, 2021

Two days after celebrating his seventy-first birthday alone, Steve calls to provide an update.

Meredith cradles the phone while I study her body language. Anything might mean everything now: a slouch, a sigh, a light trembling in the chest. A slow walk from the living room to the kitchen and back. An excusing of oneself from the room. I'm desperate for some gesture that might reveal something. An action, however imperceptible, to telegraph the tumult we've got coming. But as her father talks, Meredith's body reveals nothing. She stands, stoic, allowing the full force of his words to take root.

The call is brief, and his message is apparently uncomplicated. Meredith places the phone on the kitchen counter, then her hands on the counter beside it. In two breaths, she steadies her inner sea.

"What'd he say?" I ask.

"He said, 'I've been in a lot of pain these last couple weeks or months, so . . . so . . .' It's something he expected."

"Is he thinking hospice?"

"I think he's going to continue this last round of chemo. He's going to get a port."

Daniel Tiger's Neighborhood blares in the background—some episode involving a broken red crayon. Millie sits spellbound as Daniel works through his problem.

Meredith steers from the kitchen toward the terrarium in the dining room, where we keep the soon-to-be-monarch-caterpillars.

This is our third summer raising monarchs; our third year preparing the terrarium and attending to their needs. Each May, we insert the milkweed upon which the eggs reside. Then we await metamorphosis.

Since the butterflies are creatures Meredith can care for, she does. They have entered the pupal stage, their new weight now hanging by a thread from the top of the terrarium grate.

"How are these guys doing?" I ask, nodding to the chrysalis.

"Well, these guys"—Meredith brightens—"these guys are doing pretty well."

"They're not going to eat each other this year?"

"Mmm . . . I don't think so," she says, peering through the plastic. I peer alongside her.

"It's pretty interesting how fast they go from that to that," she says, pointing between the last egg and the first chrysalis.

"Our little guys are growing up," I say.

Silence, except for that caterwauling tiger one room over.

Meredith turns to me, her eyes placid but full. "I told my dad I'd come to Fort Wayne."

"When?"

"As soon as possible."

Reaching for our phones, we scroll through our schedules—classes and karate and camping and soccer amid the host of other obligations now cluttering our lives.

"I'm supposed to take Henry and Ellie to that reading in Dubuque on Saturday," I remind her, "so maybe you and Millie could leave before that? Or right after?"

"We'll figure it out. I just hope these guys will be okay in Fort Wayne," she says, peering into the terrarium.

"You're taking a terrarium of butterfly larvae to Fort Wayne?"

"Well, we can't just leave them here!"

"Can't we?"

She shoots me her *What kind of monster are you?* look.

"Our only problem," she says, "is whether we'll be able to find them enough milkweed to eat."

"*That's* our only problem?"

She shoots me her *Can't you just let me worry about butterflies?* look.

"What else did he say?" I ask.

"Well, he said, 'How are you?' and I said, 'Doing okay, but my dad's pretty sick,' and he said, 'Don't worry about him. He's fine.'"

I smile. It's the most Steve Ball thing Steve Ball has ever said.

"I just keep thinking about his garden," Meredith continues, her eyes now locked on the larvae. "I was so happy he planted it this year. Like it was a sign that he had faith that he'd be around for it. But if he's not . . . who will take care of it?"

"Probably not us," I say, nodding to our less-than-thriving backyard garden.

Meredith returns her attention to the chrysalises, as thin as cheesecloth, that line the top of the terrarium. For the next several weeks, they will be at the mercy of everything—one wobble, one speed bump, and they are gone. Still, they do nothing more to improve their odds of survival. They have placed their faith in their needlework. They believe in the power and the glory of a wad spooled forth from their newly discovered spinnerets. All in the hope that maybe, if the world sees fit, they might unveil themselves into their second life.

They wrap themselves in silken shrouds and wait.

What choice do we have but to wait with them?

June 2, 2021

Millie won't sleep, so we take once more to the stroller. It's a few minutes past dawn, that unbidden hour when it seems unlikeliest that humans might be roaming the world. But at least two of us are, one of whom enjoys her pretzel sticks while the other enjoys her enjoying her pretzel sticks—anything to stop the wailing.

We walk east toward the frail light, leaving the safety of our tree-lined neighborhood, toward the thoroughfare, where a couple of roundabouts direct our movement counterclockwise.

I am thinking of my father-in-law, who is no doubt awake himself, signaling the dawn of a new day by running coffee beans through the grinder. I imagine him air-pumping himself the first cup, then—following a sip—placing the blue mug on the counter-top beside yesterday's solitaire game.

Before meeting Meredith, I rarely drank coffee. But at twenty, once the Java Bean Café entered my life, every day in Fort Wayne began with a cup of Steve's. I marveled at the way he worked through the motions: measuring the beans, grinding them, and administering the precise amount of water into the dispenser to brew the cups to perfection. There was artistry involved. A technique that required some skill. Perhaps what I admired most was his unflagging commitment to the routine, which defied disruption. No matter what was happening beyond the coffee shop, within the coffee shop, there would always be a fresh pot, waiting.

In the old days, I often joked that Steve's coffee was wasted on me.

In the old days, I often joked.

At a few minutes past 6:00 a.m., Millie and I arrive at the gas station beyond the roundabouts. I enter the station for my own cup of coffee, which—as the first sip reveals—has been weakened by too much water.

Inside, a man in a paint-speckled shirt approaches the attendant and says, "I'd like to request one winning lottery ticket, please."

The attendant smiles. "I'm afraid we can't guarantee that," he says, printing the ticket.

"I understand," the man says. "Just thought I'd try."

I watch the man exit, seemingly proud of himself. I place my dollar on the counter, then rush toward the doors to catch up with him.

"Excuse me," I call. "Excuse me. Hello!"

I don't know why I do it. Who knows why we do anything?

The man turns, studying both my companion and me with skepticism.

"Yes?"

"Hi. Good morning. I just wanted to say . . . good luck with that lottery ticket."

"Oh," the man says, softening. He makes a show of folding the ticket into his breast pocket. "I was just kidding with him."

"No, I know," I say. "But still. Somebody's got to win, right?"

I wonder if he's somebody's father. Or somebody's grandfather. And if his paint-speckled shirt is some clue to the rest of his day.

"Well, I don't really need to win," he tells me. "You see, I already won the lottery once."

"Is that right?" I ask, surprised.

"Yup," he says, leaning in close for the whisper. "I found God."

We are driving to Dubuque for a backyard reading with friends. Henry and Ellie are buckled into the back seat, laughing and smiling and enjoying a reprieve from the weight of their world back home. Meanwhile, Meredith and Millie head east toward Indiana, the weight of their world compounding.

The landscape ebbs and flows like a whack-a-mole game, hill after hill, valley after valley—we can never be sure what comes next. This is the "driftless region"—a phrase having to do with ice ages, glaciers, and the sculpting of the verdant earth now stretched beyond our windshield. This landscape was forged over centuries, but we are the ones alive to reap the rewards.

Somewhere past Viroqua, the world turns wilder—the cow pastures more rugged, the barns now dotting more distant fields, and with less frequency.

"Look," Ellie shouts, extending her finger toward a field flush with light against the deciduous tree line.

"What?" I ask. "What do you see?"

"A Chosen Place!"

"A what?"

"A Chosen Place, Dad!"

I pause. It's as if she's stumbled upon some arcane knowledge.

"Where'd you hear that?" I ask.

"I made it up."

"Well, what does it mean?"

"Like a place that's chosen."

"By whom?"

"Just *chosen*."

"For what?"

"A place that's special," she explains, exasperated. "Like an *especially* special place."

That patch of land—now wedged in the rearview—indeed fits her definition.

In the distance, I begin to see what she sees: the gentle arc of the hillside unencumbered by everything but trees. Above us: the sway of shadows aligned with the overhead clouds. Even after 545 million years, it's a land left mostly bereft of hands, or hooves, or plat books. The kind of place where I'd like to build a cabin but also not build a cabin. Some places are so beautiful you can only see them once.

Henry rolls the window down further, leans forward, and feels the rush of wind catch in his curly hair. He howls as his heartbeat ping-pongs through his circuitry. Ellie joins the howling, though her shorter frame prevents her from angling her head much beyond the window. She balances her chin atop the rounded glass, squinting as the wind dries her eyes.

Blurring through the back roads, we howl so loud that a couple of cows take note.

We drive beyond the reach of our echoes. It's nice to think we left something behind.

An hour later, in a place called Dickeyville, we find Jesus entombed behind glass.

Ellie marvels at the mystery. Of all the places Jesus might've called home, how did he choose a small town in southwestern Wisconsin?

Welcome to the Grotto, a sign reads. *Gift Shop in Back.*

Since we have an hour or so before the backyard reading, we exit the car to stand before the shrine—a cave-like structure perhaps twenty feet tall and embossed in shells and stones. And pottery, and porcelain, and petrified wood. And starfish and sea urchins too. And agates. And amber glass. A bric-a-brac of most any old thing that believers believed would bring them closer to God.

"Come on," Ellie says, pulling me past the marble-cut Jesus and the gallery of saints en route to the gift shop just beyond. Which is the true wonder, as far as Ellie is concerned, because who wouldn't want a fourteen-piece nativity scene whose figurines bear a striking resemblance to toys? Bypassing the Bibles and the rosaries, she kneels before a basket of stones on sale for a quarter each.

"What's this?" she asks, holding one in her hand.

"A worry stone," I say, reading the accompanying signage. "I guess you're supposed to hold it when you're scared."

And because we are scared—and have been since Steve's initial diagnosis the previous October—it seems like a quarter well spent.

I pay the woman at the counter. I ask: "Have you ever witnessed any miracles here?"

"Miracles? Oh no." The woman laughs. "No, nothing quite like that."

Behind me, Henry loses himself in the secondhand items—donated books, cassette tapes, candles: the usual fare that washes ashore in places such as this. But Ellie remains fixated on her stone, which is not a real stone but a smooth, transparent orb of plastic with an angel figurine trapped within.

"Don't lose it," I tell Ellie as we exit the gift shop. "We're going to need it."

June 5, 2021
(continued)

Following the backyard reading, the kids and I return to the car for a few miles more on the road. Driving through the twilight, the Chosen Places emerge in full color—half a palette's worth of blues and golds splattered across the drapery of sky. Since the hour grows late, we put the pedal to the metal past the Mississippi River, then Dickeyville, then Potosi, en route to a town called Fennimore.

I've never heard of the place, but it's nearly our halfway point home. Close enough to point us in the right direction, but far enough to keep us from getting there. Which is why I booked the room.

We pull into Fennimore's only hotel a few minutes past 8:00 p.m., parking the car directly before the block-long historic structure. We cannot enter fast enough, Henry and Ellie slinging backpacks over their shoulders and ringing the front desk bell.

"Welcome, welcome!" A woman in her forties greets us. She opens her guest book and drags a finger down a row. "You must be the Hollars."

"We are," Ellie says, nodding toward the eye-level candy bowl. "Can I have some candy, please?"

"Why sure," she says. "If it's okay with your dad."

I know a losing battle when I see one.

"So what brings you to Fennimore?" the woman asks.

I mention the backyard reading.

"An author!" she says. "Well, how about that."

"It's mostly just an excuse to get away," I say.

"My grandpa," Ellie confides through a mouthful of candy, "is sick."

Henry nods solemnly.

"Oh," the proprietor says, her smile fading. "Well, I'm sure sorry to hear that."

"I love your hotel," I say, steering the conversation as far away from death as I can. "I bet it's got a great story."

"It does," she agrees. "It was built in 1918, and after the first one burned to the ground, they built it back more or less fireproof. Why don't I give you the tour?"

We roam the building, the woman showing off the adjacent bar (repurposed for continental breakfast) and an interior church, which—for reasons beyond my initial understanding—appears to have been constructed to resemble Main Street, USA.

A few dozen chairs line the patterned carpet, directed toward a makeshift stage. Just above is a storefront's exterior facade, while off to the left, an awning reads Lincoln Avenue. We gaze upon a rock garden near a dried-up stream to our right. All around us, fake plants flourish.

"So . . . this is a church?" I ask. "Right here in the hotel?"

"It used to be a dinner theater," she explains, "but we moved some things around, took out the buffet, and now it's a church. The man who originally designed this space wanted it to look like Galena, Illinois," she says. "I think he was from there."

The following morning, I wake early and take a seat in a pretend avenue near a pretend stream in pretend Galena, Illinois. Eyes closed, hands clasped, pretending.

Interview #3
Winter 2022

B.J.: What do you remember about our trip to Dubuque?

Ellie: Where?

B.J.: That time when you found all the Chosen Places.

Ellie: Oh, I liked when we went to that rock pile . . .

Henry: It's called a grotto.

Ellie: That grotto.

B.J.: Did you think about Boppy much that trip?

Ellie: No, I didn't. I also liked when we had those grilled donuts at the reading.

B.J.: What about the hotel?

Henry: They were so nice. Everyone was like, "Do you want some pizza? We have some pizza." And they had a bunch of Sunny D in mini bottles. They had a bunch of food, and they didn't care who took it. You could tell they weren't the richest hotel in the world, but they still wanted to give away everything they could.

B.J.: Remember breakfast?

Ellie: That . . . was not a good breakfast for me.

B.J.: Because you spilled the eggs?

Ellie: Yeah.

B.J.: I shouldn't have yelled.

Ellie: And then I stole your breakfast!

B.J.: That's okay. It happens.

Because time won't stop on planet Earth, we go to the one place it might. A deserted island tucked deep into Eau Claire's Chippewa River. Admittedly, we're still technically on Earth, though this spot seems otherworldly. A place with no clocks, no calendars, no time beyond the rise in the river.

I don't quite know why I've taken her here. Perhaps for the same reason I've dragged her on all my summer adventures. Whether searching for geese, grottos, or golf balls, I can never shake the feeling that this is our last chance to be together just as we are. The quiet rift has not yet begun. We are still mostly intact.

Only later will we learn what Meredith now knows: that these mostly forgettable days with your dad are actually the good days.

For the last time all summer—and perhaps ever—Ellie sits directly before me on the kayak, balancing herself as best she can as I paddle us cross-current toward the island's shore. The kayak's nose nestles into the dense shrubbery.

"Can you believe we're here?" I whisper.

"Yes," she says. "I watched you paddle the whole way."

Ellie wobbles out of the kayak, followed by me.

We dawdle in the ankle-deep water as the 90-degree sun beats down. The light refracts the ripples; our toes look bent beneath the waves.

We cut into the island's interior, where the tall trees and thick vines cloak the canopy in gauzy darkness. Lichen drapes the dead logs like lattice. The chalky rocks leave their mark on our sandaled feet. Ahead of us, we see the outlines of deer trails, and maybe human trails too. As we walk along the flinty stones, I make up a story about an antediluvian devil whose bones once washed upon these tranquil shores—not a sea creature, but close.

"Daaaadd," Ellie says, high-stepping over the clumped grass. "Stooopp."

At the heart of the island, we stumble upon the remains of a fire pit—stones, ash, and half a case of crumpled cans. A rotted wooden table, too, and beside it, a lawn chair busted back to its beginnings. Our eyes fall to a torn traffic cone tucked beneath the leaves, then onto the splintered skateboard deck.

But our most startling discovery is the rusted-to-pieces bicycle beneath the tendrilled weeds. The green of the banana seat serves as a perfect match for the foliage, which strangles the spokes. Ellie sidles toward it, lingering a body's length away. Her fear is my own: that some fork-tongued snake might slither from between its metal frame. Or worse: that the bike once belonged to some kid, maybe some kid like her, who hasn't been heard from in a while. We cannot shake the taint of some terrible deed.

"How did it get here?" Ellie asks.

"Well," I try, "the water gets low in late August. Maybe someone just walked it over."

She doesn't buy it. The bike got here by boat, or somebody swam it here—each image disconcerting for reasons we can't fully explain.

And then: a rustle from the nearby bushes.

We turn to catch a doe erupting from her hiding spot, dashing toward the hip-high weeds along the rocky shore.

"Woah!" I shout. "Woah, woah." My adrenaline shifts from terror to relief. "Did that scare you too?" I laugh.

Ellie grips my waist, though she shakes her head no.

"How did . . . the deer get over here?" she whispers.

"Maybe she rode the bike?"

For the moment, the darkness dissipates. A pair of purple salamanders scatters to the cold sides of rocks. But then, the darkness returns—clouds gather, blotting out the sun.

"Want to get off this stupid island?" I ask.

She nods.

We board the kayak and paddle along the island's shore. Just a few paddles in, I spot another Titleist 3 golf ball submerged a quarter inch into the muck.

"Are you kidding me?" I whisper, leaning over the kayak's edge to pluck it from the turbid water.

"How does this keep happening to us?" Ellie asks.

"Somebody up there must like us," I say, pointing skyward. "Or wants us to become golfers."

We smile the whole ride home, grateful that the universe has conspired to bestow us with golf balls, none of which we need or want, but it's nice to be considered.

When we pull into the drive, we see Meredith seated on the porch steps.

"What's up?" I ask.

"I talked to Boppy," she says.

Ellie and I stand in the front yard, silent as stones.

"They'll try one more transfusion," Meredith continues, "but I'll help him look for hospice when we're in Fort Wayne."

"How's he taking it?" I ask.

"He's fine," Meredith says. "I mean, not fine but . . . fine. He was a little nervous about telling me, but once he did, it got easier."

I nod.

"How'd it go for you guys?" she asks.

"We found a golf ball and four turtles!" Ellie says, holding up the accompanying number of fingers.

"What is with you guys and golf balls?" Meredith laughs.

"Ellie's going to make a great caddy one day," I say.

"Anyway, I ordered pizza," Meredith says, rising and pulling the storm door open.

I haul the kayak out of the van and lean it against the back of the house, beside our garden, which is not flourishing. Above me, our backyard crows crowd the lowest branches of the pines, filling in the gaps like shadows.

June 8, 2021

Throughout the summer, our garden's bounty comes in the form of owls. Two of whom are grounded in the dirt throughout the early summer days. The first is plastic, wide-eyed and stiffer than taxidermy—a sentinel whose sole role is to deter the wayward deer.

But since he falls short, we enlist a second owl, this one with solar-powered eyes.

Despite these measures, the invaders remain undeterred. Most days, our backyard resembles a scene from *Watership Down*: the squirrels, chipmunks, rabbit, and deer never get turned away. They view the owls as waitstaff—a friendly host and a maître d' escorting them to their table.

For a time, we grow the usual things in the garden: basil, thyme, tomatoes. But it's never enough to feed the neighborhood herd, who dip daily into whatever has sprung from the ground. Soon, the tomato vines are emptied. Soon, the herbs are too. The deer are the greatest transgressors, and I do nothing. Mostly because I prefer their presence to whatever the garden might grow. The truth is, we already have plenty of everything.

This is our year of plenty. Our year of such abundance, both good and bad, that we're crushed beneath its weight. We have gorged on so much for so long. One bite into a ripened peach, and its flavor turns to mist. Another bite into a pear, and we're rewarded with tasteless granules.

I'd like to tell you that we are focused on the garden. That

Meredith and I find solace there. We don't. We tend to it just enough to keep it from turning to ruin.

An entire world exists within the garden's four-by-four-foot chicken wire frame. The bugs drag their armored exoskeletons through the dirt while the dive-bombing robins pluck those bugs like figs. The weeds spring forth from the earth at twice the rate of the seedlings. We sigh, shrug, and take what we can get.

In a different summer, we'd keep better watch—reaching for trowels, hand rakes, and cultivator tools. Dirty our hands in the dark soil, burying our flesh from palm to tip to ensure seeds are properly planted. Would tend to the basil with monkish attention. Would spot a shriveled leaf and reach for the watering can.

But this summer, we are too caught up in human needs to consider anything else.

Several years back, when Henry was five or so and Ellie barely three, we watched a doe abandon her fawn on our lawn. The fawn was half-hidden in clover, nestled near the edge of a mostly broken fence. Throughout the day, he occasionally bobbed his nose like a dowsing rod but otherwise never moved.

To our relief, the doe returned at dusk. From the kitchen window, the kids and I watched their reunion. How she nuzzled her wobbly boy back to his hooves. How they raised their white tails like survival.

Six months later—long after the garden was gone and our owls were neck-deep in snow—I peeked out the window to spot three deer nosing their way through the hoarfrost. They were more apparition than animal. More guest than pest. I like to think they were a family. And that perhaps the littler one was the one we'd met in the clover the previous spring.

That morning when the deer returned, the world was so cold it could snap. So cold I swear I saw a shimmer of heat rising from their fur. Long after they'd left us, their hoofprints held firm in the snow. A reminder, not of what we'd lost but of all we'd been given.

{ II }

During

June 12, 2021

Since the fish must be biting somewhere, Steve's buddy Wayne loads the poles and tackle box into the back of the car.

"Wait . . . where are you guys going?" Meredith asks them.

"Chain O'Lakes," Steve says.

Which means that we all are.

Though we have only recently completed the nine-hour drive from Eau Claire to Fort Wayne, we buckle up again: this time, with Meredith's brother as well, as we make the thirty-mile drive north from our hometown to Chain O'Lakes State Park. Windows down, with Taylor Swift blaring, for a moment, things are generally good.

The park's beach overflows with Hoosiers, a few hundred of whom have gathered on this bright and young summer day. Sunscreen-slathered bodies collapse into towels, soaking in every beam. Midriffs and tan lines run amok. Freckles line faces like maps. Beyond the beach, a couple of high school kids work the boat rental hut—one accepts payment and points toward the paddles, while the other unspools seaweed from the pedal boat wheels. The visitors untether the boats' nylon ropes from the dock poles. Smiles sweep across their faces as they wave to anyone on shore willing to return the wave.

Steve and Wayne grab their gear and bypass the crowd as best they can. They veer left, weaving along the trail's edge until selecting the perfect fishing spot right where the mud meets water. Steve, who's known Wayne since elementary school, towers over his longtime friend. That Wayne flew from Arizona to spend the week here says all you need to know about him.

Loaded down with swim diapers and sand toys, I waddle toward a sliver of sand adjacent to the fishermen. Not so close that we're crowding them, but not so far away that we can't keep a careful watch.

On this day, Steve looks good. Feels good. Seems good, too. He reaches for his rod, then wades into the calf-deep water. For much of the first hour, we non-fishers cool off in Sand Lake—one of the larger lakes in the constellation of lakes for which the park is named.

Following our requisite trip through the snack bar line, Henry—sno-cone in hand—sloshes toward Boppy and Wayne.

"How's the fishing?" he asks, gnashing his teeth into shaved ice.

"Pretty good," his grandfather says.

"Can I try?"

Steve considers the logistics—three fishermen, and two poles.

"Ummm . . ."

"How about we set you up with this pole," Wayne says, handing his over. "Want me to cast it for you?"

"Okay," Henry says, finishing his treat and pocketing the wax cone.

Back on shore, I make myself invisible. Wayne, working toward the same end, joins me there.

"Thanks for the pole," I say.

"Oh, sure, sure," Wayne says. "My pleasure."

We watch Henry and Steve cast their lines awhile longer, Wayne reentering the scene only when Henry hooks a fish.

"Dad, look at this one!" Henry calls.

I give him a thumbs-up. Meanwhile, Wayne reverses the hook from the fish's mouth and then tosses the creature back to its life.

"Hey, Boppy," Henry says. "Remember that time I caught the two fish on one hook?"

"Now that was something," Steve says, his high-pitched laughter catching in the trees.

"That *was* something," Henry agrees. "I mean, two fish! One hook!"

I smile as Steve and Henry slip back into the ease of their routine, finding a silence that suits them both. Nearby, a clot of swimmers—perhaps Henry's age—plunge and breach the waterline, churning up root beer–colored wakes.

An hour later, Steve and Wayne pack their gear and head back toward the car. Meredith and I watch, having been blessed with a moment's peace. But when Steve lifts his leg toward the concrete barrier between the beach and the grass, our blessing breaks. Steve loses balance, and the world sways with him. Meredith, her brother, and I watch as his body pitches forward but does not fall. He catches himself; he finds renewed footing in the grass.

Steve continues toward the lot as if nothing has happened. Maybe, for him, nothing has. But to those of us back on the beach, the message is clear. The world will show no quarter.

Interview #4
Winter 2022

B.J.: What else?

Meredith: He felt an obligation to give blood all the time, and he'd always ride his bike there. One time he drove, and the nurses looked out the window and were like, "You have a car?" I'm pretty sure they thought he was homeless. Just a homeless guy who gave blood all the time.

B.J.: That's right. He always gave blood. I wonder why.

Meredith: I don't know. He always did, ever since I was a kid. He'd just consistently do that. However often he could.

[*Pause.*]

B.J.: I've got to start giving blood.

Meredith: You should.

June 12, 2021
(continued)

It is, thank God, a perfect night for baseball. Steve, Wayne, Meredith, Henry, and Ellie enter the minor league ballpark an hour or so before dusk. The Fort Wayne TinCaps versus the Lake County Captains in a game that no one has been waiting for. Still, it seems a good way to burn a summer night—outside among a few thousand fans.

Meanwhile, I am at my parents' house with Millie, playing some backyard game that also involves a ball. And a scoop. And a hat. And a wagon. And a whole lot of running barefoot through the backyard grass.

A few miles away, the TinCaps' bats come alive. A two-run homer in the bottom of the first put the TinCaps on the board. The Captains respond with a run in the second. But the real damage is done in the third, when a barrage of hits lifts the TinCaps to a 7–1 lead. Runners turn the chalky baselines to ruin.

Steve settles in between Ellie and Wayne, lifts his beer to his lips, then returns it to its place between his knees. He smiles. Or I imagine he smiles. A beer in the ballpark among family and friends—what more could he ask for?

Steve and Wayne small-talk their way toward the latter half of the game. They assume normalcy: cheering for the base hit and bemoaning the walk. Critiquing the ump, the coach, or anyone else in need of critiquing. That night, no one pities anyone. There is nothing in the world that a two-run homer can't fix.

"Mom," Ellie says, "can I dump the ice out of my cup?"

"Sure," Meredith says. "I'm heading to the bathroom anyway."

Together, they walk up the cement stairs toward a drain where Ellie proceeds to dump her ice.

"Go straight back to the seat with Boppy," Meredith says. "I'll be right back."

Ellie does not go straight back to her seat. She tries, but suddenly all the seats look the same. All the people, too.

"Hot dogs!" call the roving bands of vendors. "Get your hot dogs here!" Ellie shouts for her mother, but the vendors' voices carry farther than her own.

And so, she roams the ballpark. Alone. It is the first time in her young life that a trusted adult is not an arm's length away.

Meredith returns from the bathroom to find the seat beside her father empty.

"Where's Ellie?"

Steve does not know. Henry does not know. Wayne does not know, either.

The announcer calls for the next batter, and that batter steps up to the plate.

Panic sets in—acute, then throbbing. How does a seven-year-old just disappear? How does a rusted bike with a banana seat end up buried beneath an island's weeds?

Authorities are notified. The pageantry of "lost child" protocols goes into effect. Men and women with walkie-talkies share descriptions of Ellie's clothes. The stadium goes on lockdown—no one is permitted to leave. Fair-weather fans cluster around the exits. Meredith shakes. Steve rises from his seat and scans the rows around him. Suddenly, it's a less-than-perfect night for baseball.

Later, Ellie will admit that perhaps she was just a little scared. Explain how she got turned around. Got caught in the riptide of fans and vendors until she flowed into the ocean of strangers. Until, at last, a pair of security guards as tall as trees pluck her from the far side of the stadium and take her into their care.

"Come with us," the first giant says. And because he seems like a friendly giant—kind and honest and true—she takes a chance in following him.

"Sweetheart," the second giant says, "do you remember what your mother is wearing?"

"Yes." Ellie nods solemnly. "She is wearing a lime-green shirt."

Meredith is not wearing a lime-green shirt. They reunite anyway, a shaken Ellie curling into her seat alongside her grandfather.

The game groans on; the lockdown lifts.

At last, I enter the scene.

"Hello?" I say into the phone.

"Don't worry," Meredith begins. "Everything's fine now."

Relief meets rage, and anger meets exhaustion, but finally, gratitude wins.

"But . . . how did it even happen?" I ask.

"You'll have to ask her."

"Can I talk to her?"

Meredith hands Ellie the phone.

"Hi, Dad."

I asked her what happened, but of course, she doesn't know. Somehow, bad things defy simple explanations. They either happen or they don't. And when they don't, we don't even know that we've been spared.

"Well, were the security guards nice?" I ask. "The ones who found you?"

"Yup!"

"Lime-green shirt, huh?"

"Dad, I was almost sure!"

Over the past nine months, "almost sure" is a phrase I've come to know but never trust. We have been "almost sure" of many things, few of which proved true. What does prove true—what always proves true—works itself out in the rhythms of the game.

Three strikes and you're out. Four balls and you walk. What a pleasure to exist within such certainty.

Once the game ends, the fans stick around for fireworks night at the ballpark.

The thump of rockets torches the sky like mortar fire, followed by splashes of sparked rain. Each firework shimmers against the Fort Wayne skyline before evaporating.

How many times have I witnessed Steve's incomprehensible joy at sharing fireworks alongside his family? His high-pitched hyena laughs, his incessant "oohs" and "ahhs"?

From my parents' backyard, I can't quite make out the fireworks themselves, though I hear the eruptions of their distant, muffled pops.

Back at the ballpark, Meredith snaps a photo of her father and daughter caught in the gloam of stadium light.

Don't worry. Everything's fine. Now.

Safely Ashore
June 2004

The boy one bunk over asks if I know what radiation feels like.

"Not really," I say.

"It feels like this bubble," he says, "like this bubble that runs all the way through your body."

"Oh," I say.

"Like . . . have you ever seen the movie *The Mummy*?"

I nod.

"Well, there's a part where a bubble just goes through his body and . . . that's pretty much like radiation."

"Oh," I say again.

It's 11:00 p.m., and we're supposed to be asleep. As their camp counselor, I should know better. But already, it's become apparent to those of us in the cabin that there are plenty of things that I don't know. I am surrounded by a quartet of ten-year-old cancer survivors who have come to this place following their harrowing ordeal.

I am twice their age and have never had cancer. I know nothing of harrowing ordeals.

Flashlight beams bounce shadows off the cabin's paint-slapped walls. It's the same cabin where, a decade ago, I, too, bounced shadows against those walls.

"Not a lot of people really know what it feels like to be dying," says the boy in the bunk to my left.

"What does it feel like?" I ask.

"Well, it's like being alive, only . . . you notice things."

"What kind of things?"

"All things," he says. "Like, there are three spiderwebs above my bed right now. And there are sixteen nails in the cabin ceiling. Oh, and five candy wrappers in the trash can. And a bird's nest beneath the lodge steps."

"You noticed all of that?"

"You have to, or you feel like you have to," he says. "One morning, I woke up and thought, 'I could be dead before the end of the day.'"

The other three boys in the bunks nod alongside him.

"All right, guys," I say. "Flashlight off. Let's hit the hay. Got a big day tomorrow."

For a moment, the room turns silent, and then:

"B.J.?"

"Hmm?"

"There are two fireflies in the cabin," the camper says.

He doesn't want me to do anything about them. He just wants me to know that they're there.

————

Seventeen summers before Steve dies of cancer, I sit in the lodge and listen to the childhood cancer survivors chat about the disease that nearly took their lives. Steve's daughter Meredith, whom I've met two weeks prior, sits with her campers just a few tables down. I am not yet in love with her, but almost. Over the next few weeks, we will fall into the practice of leaving each other notes in our mailboxes—swoops and scrawls folded into the tiniest squares. We make each other bracelets in the art barn. She leaves spiraled orange peels in my backpack just because.

The morning after the spiders, while eating blueberry pancakes, the campers explain to me that you never really "beat cancer." That the best you can do is beat it back. They rattle off facts about red blood cells and white blood cells while asking me to please pass the syrup.

"Hey, what did you guys do when you were getting chemo?" one camper asks, his mouth overflowing with pancakes.

Two say they played video games. The other says he hummed his favorite song.

The boy who asked the question stays quiet until the question is turned back toward him.

"One time, I had the mask over my face—you know the mask with the tiny slits?"

The others nod.

"So I'm sitting there, lying there I guess, when all of a sudden I see these kids above me. They're staring down at my face and . . . and they're laughing."

The nodding stops.

"And it's so weird because I can't move, I'm just frozen there and . . . I can feel them pulling at my skin, trying to tear the cancer away from me. I saw them all the time. During chemo, I mean."

Silence.

"The ghosts don't leave you," he continues. "Sometimes the cancer leaves, but the ghosts don't. Even now, when I close my eyes, I can see them."

Across the lodge, Meredith laughs alongside her campers, joy splashing across her face like sunscreen.

It is morning. The flags have been raised. For seventeen years, we will bask in that light.

June 16, 2021

It feels wrong to make the call while he is still here; still, I reach for my phone. A naturalist from Pokagon State Park answers.

"Hi," I say. "I'm hoping to purchase a memorial bench. For my father-in-law."

"Of course," the woman says. "I'm sorry for your loss."

"Well, we haven't lost him yet," I explain. "We are still losing him."

I explain to the naturalist that he has small cell lung cancer. Stage four. Her silence confirms that this is more information than she requires.

"Anyway," I say, pacing the garden on the backside of Steve's coffee shop, "I guess I'm just trying to be proactive."

"Of course," she says. "We have a third-party vendor that makes the benches. I can email you the information if you like."

"Sure," I say. "I guess the only part that matters is that we need a spot on the lake. Steve, my father-in-law, is a fisherman. He just wants a bench so fellow fishermen can untangle their lines. So we need a place within casting distance. If that's possible."

The naturalist turns quiet. I imagine her standing beside the terrariums in the park's nature center, which we visit annually—or did. I see her standing before the observation window foregrounding the hundreds of birds and squirrels nibbling at the feeders.

"I'm sorry," she says at last. "We're out of lakefront spots for memorial benches. They're quite popular . . ."

I don't hear what she says next. All I hear is my heart pounding in my head.

"I understand," I say. "But, you see, he's dying. This is his last wish. I've been asked to carry out this last wish. I'm his son-in-law. I need to believe there's some patch of land, just a couple of feet, where a bench might fit. Please. We go there every summer."

"Yes, but—"

"He's probably caught half the fish in that lake," I say. "Please."

Because the naturalist can't bear to say no, she agrees to take it up with the property manager.

Behind me, Steve walks slowly from the coffee shop to the house.

I hang up and slip the phone into my pocket.

"Morning, Steve," I say.

"Hi."

He shuffles out of view while I collapse in a lawn chair and watch the flies swarm the unripe tomatoes.

Eyes closed, I refine my argument, brainstorming how best to guilt-trip a naturalist and a property manager into granting us a lakefront memorial bench. A bench where people might untangle fishing lines, feed a few geese, and chat idly with their grandchildren. A place where people might fall in love, or, if they're not careful, perhaps in the lake.

Hours later, I receive an email from the naturalist. She informs me that she has spoken with the property manager, who has agreed to the request.

"Ted, our manager, is a fisherman who appreciated your story about untangling the fishing line," the naturalist writes. "He said there is a space along the lake, down the stairs from campground 1, near the fishing dock. How does that sound?"

This is the one time I weep.

June 16, 2021
(continued)

On the backside of the coffee shop, peering out at his garden, Steve turns to Ellie and says, "So are you getting into any trouble these days?"

Sensing a trap, Ellie measures her next words carefully.

"Um . . . I don't know," she says. "I don't think I'm getting into too much trouble."

What she wants to say is: *I love you, I love you, I love you. And I miss you even though you're still here.*

I can't know this for sure, but I am as sure of it as anything. Because I have known my own daughter for seven years. And because when I was seven, after the death of my grandfather, I, too, stopped saying aloud those things I most desperately wanted. For me, this manifested in an addendum to every nightly prayer. After my rote recitation of "Now I lay me down to sleep," I'd say, "I hope nobody dies tonight." Throughout elementary school, I'd toss my prayers into paper airplanes and send them soaring. Or when flying a kite, I'd imagine the prayers making their way to someone up in the clouds. Thirty years later, I'm still adding that addendum. I know it won't be answered, but I've grown accustomed to the nightly rituals: like prayer, like the coffee shop, like fishing.

Steve sits back in his chair, pondering the problem of his granddaughter's good behavior.

"Well, you've got a bicycle now, right?" Steve asks her. "I bet you can get into trouble with that."

Ellie considers it.

"You could always ride it and get ice cream," Steve suggests. "That might get you in trouble."

"We do like riding our bikes to get ice cream," I say from my place one seat to his left.

"There you go," Steve says. "Sounds like a plan."

Silence, then, as we watch the tomatoes.

"Do you have any questions you'd like to ask Boppy?" I ask Ellie.

"Um . . ." She ponders. "What was your farthest bike ride?"

"My farthest bike ride," he says matter-of-factly, "was from Fort Wayne to Cleveland. I also rode from here to Bloomington once. And I did Washington, DC, to Ocean City. Pittsburgh to DC, too, I guess. That was nice. You should make your dad do that with you sometime."

Ellie turns toward me for confirmation that perhaps someday we can.

"Well, I can finally change bike tires with some regularity," I say, "so now there's no stopping us."

"I can do that," Steve says. "I just did that, actually."

Just? I think.

"I'll tell you what," Steve says, lifting his eyebrows, "that bike that I've got, you should steal that, B.J."

"It's a good bike," I say.

"It's a great bike," he corrects me.

"Well, I'd put some miles on it, that's for sure."

"Good," Steve says, "I hope you do."

This is the second to last moment Steve and I are alone together. Alone with Ellie, at least, who serves as the perfect buffer to ensure that neither of us feels compelled to say too much. I have no problem disclosing to a naturalist whom I've never met the details of my father-in-law's decline, but the prospect of discussing such details with the man himself is more than either of us can bear.

Gripping both sides of the lawn chair, Steve rises, then walks toward the detached garage behind the shop. He removes a key from his pocket, unlocks the garage, enters that darkness, and retrieves the bike, which he rolls into the noonday sun.

"Yup, Boppy's got the coolest bike," I announce to Ellie. "No doubt about that."

"Lift it," he says.

I do, with one hand.

"Well?"

"It's the lightest thing on earth," I say.

Steve nods.

Meredith pulls up with the takeout barbecue.

"Uh oh." She smiles. "What's he up to now?"

"Just showing off this awesome bike I'm going to steal," I say. "I'll probably have to lower the seat, though. Like . . . a lot."

"Is he leaving it to you?" she asks, turning toward her father. "Dad, should we put it in the will?"

(These days, this is what passes as a joke.)

"Sure," he agrees, wheeling the bike back into the dark garage.

Ellie peeks her head into the garage as Steve returns the bike to its place beside the bucket of ice fishing gear.

"I got beef brisket," Meredith says cheerily. "Eat as much as you want."

"I hate beef brisket," Steve says, returning outside.

"I didn't know you hated beef brisket!"

"In your whole life," Steve says, "you have never seen me eat brisket."

June 17, 2021

Ahead of us, the white storks tiptoe through the knee-high reeds, paying us little mind. They are at home in their habitat. At home with the other zoo-goers, much like us, who are anxious to capture a photograph of what we plainly see.

Henry is away at summer camp, so the rest of us—Meredith, the girls, and my parents too—spend a morning at the Fort Wayne Children's Zoo. I've been coming here for decades. In the old days, I could often be found dawdling on the far side of the sea lions' glass: mesmerized as those oily-skinned creatures shimmered against the broken rays of light, engaged in what appeared to be play. As a child, my grandfather often accompanied me here, hunkering low on his bum knee, shouting, "Now how do you like that?" every time any animal did anything. For a time, my grandfather was the oldest person I ever knew. But he was spry and a trickster, too—perpetually hiding loose change beneath the couch cushions so I'd always have something to find. Once, I came upon him napping barefoot on the couch and was stunned by the thick callouses he'd accumulated. The pads of his feet were their own pedometer—each groove and ridge its own story.

On this day, my parents fulfill the grandparents' role, watching the girls as we enter the African Journey portion of the zoo. A soft mist hisses from the sprinkler heads, coating and cooling our bodies. We slow-walk through it. For a moment, we all but disappear.

A quarter century ago, back in fifth grade, my class had a lock-in at this zoo. My classmates and I packed pillows and sleeping bags, then bedded down across from the reticulated python. But before we slept, we received a nocturnal tour of those animals we might not fully see in daylight. We watched as a cage full of owls roused themselves awake and a bat-eared fox shook from slumber. But because merely observing animals wasn't educational enough, our teachers also asked us to complete a writing assignment.

Pick an animal and write a poem—that was the prompt.

Around 10:00 p.m., I positioned myself alongside a Komodo dragon, then flipped to a fresh page in my notebook. I refused to reduce him to metaphor. But I struggled to think up much of anything else to say about him, either. Instead, I tried to catch his attention. I waved my arms to persuade that creature to notice me with the same fervor I was noticing him. He ignored me like a white stork. I wrote a poem anyway.

That night, before my classmates and I bedded down beside the python habitat, a few friends and I stumbled upon a row of "mystery boxes," into which, according to the signage, we were meant to stick our hands. Something about the power of touch, the sign informed us. Something about the senses. My friends did it, so I felt compelled to do it too. My fingers trembled as I reached beyond the rubber flaps, grazing shell, and feather, and bone. The fourth box contained a snakeskin, perhaps from the python who eyed us behind his glass. That's when I decided I'd had quite enough mystery boxes, refusing to reach within that fifth and final box.

Today, that python is dead. Those boxes are gone. That poem, too, has vanished.

There is a time in your life when you will outlive almost every animal in the zoo, and another time when you won't outlast the mist.

If asked to write that poem today, this is where I'd begin.

High-stepping through the low-growth bramble in my parents' backyard, Ellie and I approach the graves. We are en route to our family's pet cemetery, which, over the past two decades, has dramatically increased in the number of graves. What was once home to a cat is now home to two dogs, several cats, a handful of hamsters, a pair of gerbils, and a guinea pig. My father, a gravedigger by trade, dug every hole himself.

Growing up, we rarely journeyed to this section of property—a shock of forest abutting a major road. Over time, the vegetation reclaimed the path from the house to the burial markers, most of which were positioned haphazardly like broken teeth. The path vanished so slowly that no one noticed until it was gone—swallowed up by sticker bushes and a tangle of ferns.

But on this day, beneath the burning sun, Ellie and I bypass the overgrown path in favor of the one running parallel to it. The electric company recently cleared the way for power lines, and in doing so, reclaimed it from the wild, providing us new access to the all-but-forgotten graves.

"Do you know the way?" I ask Ellie.

"Sure," she says. "Follow me."

No matter that she's never been there in her life. She is a four-foot-tall divining rod, her body veering across the crumbled dirt until a slight opening emerges on the right side of the path. Bypassing the thickets of crabgrass and thistle, I return to a place I feared I'd lost for good.

The overhead branches dapple shadows on the stone markers just ahead. How strange, the way earth grows dark in broad daylight.

"See this one?" I say, crouching alongside the freshest grave. "This is Cinder the cat. You remember Cinder, right?"

"You found her in a car engine," she says. "Her whispers were singed."

"Her *whiskers*," I correct. "And I didn't find her. Grandpa did. But yeah, that's pretty much right. And this one," I say, continuing our tour, "is Sydney the dog. And Pumpkin the dog's right here beside her. And Morris the cat right here."

"Wait—how did Cinder die again?"

"Grandma and Grandpa had to take her to the vet. She was old and coughing a lot."

A worried look washes over her.

"Sometimes I cough a lot," she says.

"This was a different kind of cough. She was having a hard time breathing."

Ellie crouches to examine a roly-poly pill bug, prodding it with her finger until it curls into a sphere atop the soggy ground.

"If I accidentally step on you," she tells the bug, "you'd die here, too, huh, guy?"

I steel myself for the next question. "So how are you feeling about all this Boppy stuff?"

"I feel sad because I'll miss him when he's gone."

"It's going to be hard to drive home on Sunday," I say. "To say goodbye and drive you and Henry home."

Which is, indeed, our plan. Meredith and Millie will stay for "the duration" while I'll drive the older two back to Eau Claire. We have a camping trip scheduled. And soccer games. And a life that might still be waiting for us. But before all that, we still have two days and three nights together in Fort Wayne. No matter how we spend them, they'll feel squandered.

"Sunday's gonna stink," Ellie says, giving the pill bug one last poke.

"But we can't just think about the goodbye," I say. "We have to remember all the hellos before the goodbye."

All those walks to Zesto's ice cream shop. All those cups of coffee, those hands of cards, those perfectly peppered egg sandwiches. All those peeled grapefruits, backyard fires, and berries plucked from the lattice. The Chuck Mangione records. The fish fries. The Monday night dinners. The Tuesday night strolls.

"You know my grandparents used to live here," I say, pointing back to what is now my parents' house. "This was their property first. They designed the house and raised their whole family here. It's where Grandma grew up. And then when they died, your grandma and grandpa moved here, and Uncle Bri-Bri and I grew up here, too. Our family's formed a lot of memories here."

Like when my grandpa and I tromped through the property's woods in the opposite direction of this pet cemetery. How we veered right instead of left, pushing through the thorny bramble until a sunken tennis court appeared in a neighbor's backyard. Stacked railroad ties outlined the edge of the court, which, even then, was fast approaching decrepitude. A sagging net. Paint-faded lines. And enough acorns in the doubles alleys to all but ensure a rolled ankle. My grandfather first took me there when I was Ellie's age, revealing a piece of the world I never knew existed.

That day, my grandpa cracked a fresh can of tennis balls, tilting it toward my nose so I could smell their strange rubbery scent. He handed me a ball and told me to hit it. After a couple of attempts, I did. Bum knee and all, he thwacked those balls with me for half an hour or so. Together, we pulverized the acorns beneath our feet.

When it was done, we scaled those stacked railroad ties and headed back toward the house. We entered through the back door near the brown freezer, whose frosty shelves were reserved for desserts. From its lower shelf, he pulled forth our plunder: a tub of raspberry sherbet with walnuts. He carried it into the kitchen, dispensing three scoops each into a pair of flower-embossed bowls.

A few years back, the last time I made the trek to the pet cemetery, I'd stumbled across a Titleist 3 golf ball—the first of many Ellie and I would soon find. But this wasn't any old golf ball. This one belonged to my grandfather, who stuck a tee into the backyard grass, then drove that very ball into these very woods. A quarter century after his death, I plucked it from the earth. I held in my hand what he once held in his hand.

Brushing the dirt from its dimples, I thought of a story my mother once shared. How, mere hours after my grandfather's death, she discovered my grandmother distractedly folding laundry in the bedroom where my grandfather had died. My grandmother was folding her dead husband's shirts and piling them atop the bed.

"Everything okay?" my mother asked my grandmother.

"Yes," my grandmother said.

Then—because it was what she had always done, and what she'd trained her hands to do—she returned my grandfather's shirts to their proper place in the drawer.

June 18, 2021

Rain clatters atop the van roof. White-knuckled, I drive beneath the overpass. Outside, the morning looks like night. The windshield wipers cannot wipe fast enough. I am the only one dumb enough to be driving. But I have places to be.

Drenched, I enter through the coffee shop's back door. A few old-timers have already returned to their posts—the stool, the couch, the high-top chairs—busily trading small talk. Steve slumps on the couch near the picture window, his eyes closed, hands clasped behind his head. Steve's buddy Wayne lingers near the counter, clutching a cold cup of coffee in prayer. For the past week, he's accompanied Steve on nearly daily fishing trips to all their favorite lakes, offering his friend a steady stream of adventures that we are not calling a bucket list. Most afternoons, they return with a cooler full of bluegill—ostensibly for some future fish fry.

But on this morning, there are no fishing trips. We can't blame the weather. Wayne's plane for Arizona leaves in a couple of hours. Steve's cast his last line.

Shortly before nine thirty, the rain stops, and a parade of people enters. They have come for one more cup of coffee in what we are not calling a farewell party.

Forty or so gather in a shop that can comfortably hold half that.

Steve perks up at the sight of them. His smile returns. He asks his friends what they want to drink, but everyone helps themselves.

One after another, the men make their way toward Steve, coming humbly with halfhearted jokes and keeping the conversation light. They toss a couple of bucks on the counter, but in keeping tradition, no one pays much attention to who owes what. In the end, it will all work out or it won't.

Eventually, a regular named Jim asks for everyone's attention.

"It'll just take a second," he promises. "I'd just like to say a few words about my good friend Steve Ball."

Jim says what everyone has long felt. That the Java Bean Café created a place for them. A place to gather. A place to talk. A place to "give their wives a break." For years, the shop has been their daily pilgrimage. Come for the cup of coffee, sure, Jim says, but stay for the camaraderie.

For seventeen years, I'd seen it firsthand. Witnessed how Steve's coffee shop had served as a clubhouse for people who didn't have clubhouses. Not a country club, but an anti–country club. A place where drip coffee reigned supreme. A place where you could order a mocha, but no one did. It was the one place in town where you could get out of the cold on Christmas morning. If you were hungry, and it was Tuesday, Steve might make you an egg sandwich. Or offer you a bowl of oatmeal. If you wanted anything else, "tough luck for you," he'd say.

Jim is spinning in memories until finally, he finds his ending.

"Let's give it up for our good friend Steve Ball," Jim says, lifting his coffee cup high.

Cheers erupt as a few loose tears catch in the rivulets of wrinkled faces.

These men have come not only to mourn Steve's impending death but also, quietly, their own. After today, the coffee shop's doors will remain locked. The neon Open sign will darken. Next Christmas, the widowers will have nowhere to go.

Meredith watches from the far side of the shop, holding Millie to her chest like a second heart. Meanwhile, Henry and Ellie make themselves small, searching for where to put Maryland in a puzzle of the United States.

How to explain what happens next? How a lifetime's worth of friends gathers to say goodbye, shuffling toward the leader of their club. Their faithful grinder of coffee beans. The maker of egg sandwiches. The man who always read the newspaper first so he could deliver the news.

No one says, "See ya next time." Instead, they say, "You take care."

For the first time, during this last togetherness, there is no bullshit for them to hide behind.

One by one, their numbers dwindle. The sound of the weighted door closing again and again.

As the crowd dissipates, Wayne makes his way toward the couch.

"Well, Steve," he says, "I better get going myself. The plane and all . . ."

"Let me walk you out."

"Nah, you don't—"

"Let me walk you out, Wayne," Steve says irritably. He lifts himself from the couch unassisted, then walks toward the shop's back door. Meredith trails them with the baby.

From the narrow window, I watch as two men who have been friends for over sixty years chat beneath the eaves alongside the garage.

Wayne maintains his firm smile, nodding and trying for a laugh. His hands are so deep in his pockets that it's as if he's trying to pull himself in.

Eventually, the talking subsides as a new silence envelops them. There it is again, that thousand-yard gaze, now affixed to Wayne's face.

The old friends find themselves ensnared in the awkward mechanics of trying to say goodbye. Are they to hug or shake hands? What is the protocol? Where is the script? In the end, they manage a little of both before parting ways.

Later, Meredith tells me what really happened. How what I'd witnessed from the narrow window was only half of it.

Wayne began to cry, and her father stopped him.

"It'll be fine, Wayne," Steve assured his friend, walking toward the shop. "It'll be fine."

Interview #5
Winter 2022

B.J.: Can you tell me about the coffee shop?

Meredith: Well, my dad bought the coffee shop when I was in high school, but it was at a different location, way farther away. I worked there for a while back when he had employees. When I was a senior in high school, he moved it to where it was on Broadway. He opened it every morning. He only worked for five or six hours, and then he did whatever he wanted in the afternoon. Took a nap, or played handball, or went for a bike ride. He always had to do something.

B.J.: Any best memories from the shop?

[*Pause.*]

Meredith: Well, I mean, we got engaged there. That was good.

B.J.: [*Laughs.*] I'm surprised you brought that up.

Meredith: I don't know. It was always good. I remember back when Henry was young, and all the guys would be so excited to see him. Joe and Leo. Everyone would ask him questions. It was fun.

We had all those nights where we'd have "beer tastings," which were really just drinking too much beer . . . My dad would always make his food for those, and he was a really good cook.

B.J.: Shall we talk about the food?

Meredith: Potatoes. He had some awesome potatoes. He fried them in the mornings, and for those beer tastings. He would use Italian dressing on individual potatoes, and we'd dip them into this homemade dip. He liked to make his egg sandwiches. Horseradish and Miracle Whip. And his fajitas. He had a lot of different things. Pretty much anything he cooked I liked.

B.J.: Remember how, at the old house, in the early days, he'd have a fire like every night of the summer. And he'd listen to NPR jazz and drink his Moosehead. I remember thinking that it looked pretty perfect.

Meredith: And he had his hot tub.

B.J.: Right. And he seemed to really enjoy stealing berries from the neighbors' yards.

Meredith: When we'd go on walks, he'd always know where there were berries. He liked white mulberries. Those were exciting finds for him. If there were peaches, pears, or apples, he'd always go for those, too.

June 18, 2021
(continued)

Shortly after dusk, we descend barefoot into my parents' backyard. Henry holds the glass jar while Ellie trails with the net. I follow a few steps behind them both, watching as the last gasps of sunlight catch in the uppermost branches of the trees.

Decades ago, my brother and I had been the ones in search of fireflies—what else was there to do on a Tuesday in June in Fort Wayne? Decades before that, my mother and her siblings had come to the same conclusion—reaching for their own jar and net. That my children are the third generation of firefly catchers in this back-yard seems incomprehensible.

Henry spots a flash and leaps toward it with the jar.

"No, Henry!" Ellie yells at her brother's failed attempt. "That's my job. I'm the one with the net!"

"There was no time!" Henry says. "There was just no time!"

Already, my crack team is crumbling.

"Okay, let's regroup," I say. "There will be other fireflies, I promise."

Once, during my own firefly-catching nights, I'd holed up in a grove of ten-foot-tall hedges positioned precisely where we are now. I'd squeezed my body into a gap between the tallest two, hun-kering into a hollowed section invisible to outsiders. At the time, that hedge cavern had seemed like an endless network of tunnels connecting the yard's shrubbery. I followed the squirrel trails as far as I could, only reemerging when I heard my grandfather calling my name.

"Why is this so hard?" Henry grumbles, scanning the twilight.

"It used to be easier," I say. "In the old days, the fireflies were everywhere."

The children stare at me as if I've just informed them that I'm 107 years old.

"I'm serious. We didn't even need a net. We'd cup our hands, and they'd fly right in . . ."

"Sure, Dad," Henry mocks. "You'd just 'cup your hands.'"

"There's one!" Ellie calls, coiling her body before leaping—and coming up empty. Peering inside the butterfly net, she wonders how such a sure thing turned to ruin.

A few miles away, Meredith tends to her father, whose appetite has decreased significantly. Still, they flip through cookbooks together, Steve requesting meal after meal that he likely won't eat. But for him, the joy is in the page-flipping. He and his daughter sit on a couch, devouring each feast with their eyes.

They both understand that they are past the point of fixing anything. They both understand that there is nothing left to be fixed. All Meredith and her father have left to do is demonstrate devotion. Take care of each other in the modest ways they can. Flip pages. Discuss recipes and the memories they spur. Recount the past one last time. Talk about everything that came before, but never a word of what comes next.

"All right, guys, we gotta catch one," I tell the kids. "This is getting embarrassing."

"Look at that one light up its butt!" Ellie giggles, giving chase.

My mother joins the hunt, appearing in her white nightgown like some apparition roaming the Indiana moors.

"Didn't this used to be easier?" she asks me.

"That's what I said!"

After much heartache and a few scraped knees, Henry catches a single firefly and deposits it into the jar. But seeing it there, blinking into the glassy void, confirms for him that a single bug won't do.

"We need to find him a friend," Henry says, handing the net to his sister.

Fifteen minutes later, a pair of fireflies light up the jar. We've done it. We've apprehended two fireflies. Even together, they emit no more than a smudge of light.

A minute passes. Then two.

"Well?" my mom says. "Is it about time to release them?"

"Already?" Henry asks.

Begrudgingly, he unscrews the lid and awaits liftoff. But they refuse. He taps the jar, then gives it a slight shake.

"Gertrude wants to go, but Gerbert doesn't," he announces.

"You named them?"

He nods.

"When could you have possibly named them?"

"Just now."

"Who's who?"

"Gertrude is the one who wants to go," Ellie explains. "But Gerbert doesn't."

Henry confirms that she is correct.

Gertrude makes her move, at which point Henry flips the jar and pats it against his palm. "Sorry, Gerbert, time to go."

"But he doesn't want to!" Ellie says, grabbing the jar. "He can make his own decisions, Henry!"

A tug-of-war ensues as the fireflies hold their positions.

"Ellie," I say. "Don't you think he wants to be with his friends?"

"But aren't *we* his friends?"

"Not really," I say. "He probably thinks we've come to kill him."

"Is it true, Gerbert?" Ellie asks, peering into the jar. "Do you really want to leave?"

Across town, Steve and his daughter enjoy a bowl of barley soup.

One flies off, and then the other.

June 19, 2021

At 7:58 a.m., the kids and I languish in the minivan, waiting for the train to pass. It is not the first train that has stopped us this trip, nor will it be the last. The number of trains that have stalled our attempts to get to Steve's house has become a tragicomedy.

Seven minutes pass, and we go nowhere. The kids peer out at the factory off to our left. To our right: a gas station. Just ahead: a stream of train cars churning in slow motion.

Once, I had more patience. But the older I get, the less time I have for trains.

"Dad?" Ellie asks.

"Yeah?"

"Why is this train so long?"

"Because the world's trying to teach me a lesson."

"What?"

"I don't even know anymore."

Two weeks prior, after dropping the kids off at summer camp, Meredith and I had found ourselves at the mercy of a different train. Only then, we were at a middle-of-nowhere crossroad between cornfields, and still, we got stuck. We rerouted again and again, but that train stretched for the entirety of Indiana, cutting us off at every pass. There was no way around it. No way through. We might've parked the van and had a picnic. I wish we would have now.

The kids, who still have time for trains, sing along to an Olivia Rodrigo song they've heard a thousand times before. They self-soothe. They demonstrate to me that patience is a virtue. Under most conditions, they're right.

I close my eyes and will that train forward. To pass the time, I imagine this train a hundred years into the future: screeching into some scrapyard where it will rest back to its bones. A hundred years, even in train time, seems a long time. Whereas seventy-one years in human time now seems short.

June 19, 2021
(continued)

On our final morning in Fort Wayne, Ellie, my father, and I reach once more for the butterfly net. We are at some off-the-grid nature preserve across from the cemetery where my grandparents are buried. The place where, one day, my parents might be buried too.

We roam the preserve's hundred acres, eventually finding our way toward the two-acre pond on the fringes of the old-growth oaks. It is a nearly perfect replica of every pond I've ever seen, fringed with lily pads and moss. And maybe, if we're lucky, home to a bullfrog too.

Ellie tiptoes toward the water, where the mud sucks the cattails deep.

"You sure you want to step on that log?" I ask, eyeing her shoes.

"Of course," she says.

She shifts her weight to the log, and in an instant, her right shoe sloshes directly into the muck. I sigh. She shrugs. My dad smiles.

We have all assumed our roles in a morality play on the obstinance of youth.

Upon reaching the far side of the pond, Ellie spots a big-as-her-fist bullfrog buried up to its eyeballs in mud. Ellie turns toward my dad, who nods—he sees it too.

They stand statuesque, lulling it into a stupor, until she finally makes her move. She slams the net atop its slippery skin. The frog plunges, pulling its body through the cool sludge toward safety. My

dad attempts a different tactic, splashing his hands into the water and catching air.

Mud-caked and bullfrog-less, their frustration turns to laughter within seconds.

Next time! they say like thwarted villains. *Next time!*

Ellie and my dad dawdle throughout the walk back toward the van. They stop to study everything: animal, mineral, plant. Every inch of the trail reveals some new mystery. This world of ours, they determine, is baffling. We bestow everything with a genus and a species, but knowing the name of a thing is not knowing it.

My phone rings, so I leave them to their newly discovered snail.

"Hey, what's up?"

"Hey," Meredith says. "Can you help me move my dad's mattress up the stairs? The hospice bed should be arriving soon."

"Sure. Like now?"

"Like soon."

"Okay."

A pause as we determine who will say the next thing and what that next thing is.

"So . . . how's it going out there?" she asks.

"Fine," I say, "just checking out a snail currently. It appears to have suction-cupped itself to a leaf."

"I see," she says. "Well, be sure to keep me posted. On the snail."

"Absolutely."

I slip the phone back into my pocket.

"Who was that?" my father asks.

"Meredith. She needs help moving Steve's mattress up the stairs. To make room for the new bed."

"New bed?" my dad asks.

"Hospice bed," I clarify.

The rest of the walk back, Ellie scrapes her muddy shoes against every rock en route to the van. Her shoes still leave prints on the floor mats, an impenetrable Rorschach test.

"Sorry," Ellie whispers.

"It's okay," I say.

My father sits shotgun. We drive past the cemetery toward home.

We are in desperate need of a drink, so we retreat to the brewery one door down from the coffee shop. Henry and Ellie are occupied, meaning Meredith and I are accompanied only by one-year-old Millie, who is an ideal distraction. We snag an outdoor table beside the busy street. We smile when the waitress walks by. And we smile at the patrons who smile at Millie, which seems like the right thing to do.

This is not a pity party, but the closest thing to it. We study the menu with interest. We place our orders in the hopes that the words coming out of our mouths make sense. In an instant, two foam-lipped sweaty glasses appear directly before us.

"Thank you," we say to the waitress already a dozen feet away.

We take the glasses in our hands, rubbing our thumbs against the moisture to clear windows. Meredith and I sip the beers, which taste like pine needles, then watch as the amber carbonation rises before vanishing into the foam. No toasts are tendered or received. We have already said everything twice.

In the time between the drink hitting our lips and our glasses hitting the table, we are nearly normal. Returned to a time when grabbing a drink together might simply be a thing to do. Millie is perched on her mother's lap, watching the cars drive past.

When our glasses are nearly empty, we, too, turn our attention to the cars. My eyes fall to the tree across the street that saved our lives. Or if not saved our lives, then at least gave the drunk drivers a place to crash that wasn't directly into our car.

This was fifteen years prior, on a Saturday night in the fall. Meredith and I—barely boyfriend and girlfriend then—were driving down Broadway when a stolen security van crossed into our lane. I didn't think, I swerved. The van swerved too, careening into my side of the car before ricocheting toward the tree across the street. The van struck the tree and crumpled, accordion-style, like a cartoon. The boys inside—not even of driving age—stumbled forth from its various doors.

I was twenty-two. And so furious by the actions that had nearly killed us that I trembled while searching for someplace within myself large enough to hold my rage. I could not. I stared, stunned, as four boys spilled forth from the van in all directions. Hopped from a window. Popped through the back. Pulled themselves through the passenger-side sliding door. I don't remember faces, only lights—headlights, emergency lights, and the blue fog of the overhead streetlights. Blaring on the radio, and forever locked into my mind—Def Leppard's "Pour Some Sugar on Me."

I was shaken from my stupor by a voice off to my left—a little garbled, a little slurred.

"Hey, hey, man," the voice said.

I turned to face the driver—fifteen or so—dangling an unlit cigarette between his tarred fingers.

"Hey, hey man," the voice repeated. "You got a light?"

I could not make sense of his question. I heard it, but it did not make sense. It would be inaccurate to say that my *life* flashed before my eyes. What flashed before my eyes was my future. And it didn't "flash" exactly but developed slowly, like a photograph unspooled from an instant camera.

Within minutes, perhaps even before the police, Meredith's father arrived on the scene. Steve was calm and steady in the wake of crises, and I felt my fury dissipate. One look from him to me, and we shared something like gratitude. Rejoiced in the half-inch difference between life and death that, on this night, teetered in our favor. If Steve said something to me that night, I don't remember what. But I do remember how it felt just having him there. The way he surveyed the damage and saw grace in the pooling motor oil. And second chances in the plumes of engine smoke.

Fifteen years later, Steve snores on a couch just across the street from the crash, awaiting the delivery of his hospice bed.

That afternoon at the brewery, I reflect on the fickle nature of futures. The half inches here and there that spare us or don't. I gaze toward Millie—who knows nothing of tragedy yet—and pray that all the half inches always teeter her way (though I know full well they won't).

"I bought ham hocks," Meredith says. "For bean soup."

"Yeah," I say, "your dad mentioned that."

"Mentioned what?"

"Just that you'd bought a bunch of ham hocks." I shrug.

"What'd he say?"

"I don't know. He just didn't seem too happy about it."

"But what'd he *say*?"

"He said, 'I'm dying of stage four cancer. How many ham hocks does she think I'm going to eat?'"

Sighing, Meredith clasps her hands around her glass. "He's a hard man to please these days."

Following the frog hunt earlier that afternoon, I'd helped finagle Steve's former mattress up the stairs. It was more difficult than I expected. With every push up every stair, I tried to persuade myself that I was performing some kindness. That I was not complicit. That all I was doing was a thing in need of doing, so I did it.

Peering into the foam of my empty glass, I imagine Steve waking on the couch to notice that his bed has gone missing. Soon to be replaced by a different bed. A bed he does not want but needs.

I take a final sip and place my empty glass on the table.

"Ready?" I ask.

"Ready," Meredith says.

We are not.

In the Adobe Hotel in Santa Fe
January 3, 2017

We retreated into the country to try to feel less alone. This was in January 2017—months after an election had cleaved the country in two. Feeling alone was one of our more manageable emotions, one we soothed with margaritas in the adobe hotel near downtown Santa Fe. Meredith and I had never been anywhere near New Mexico, so we booked the flight, enlisted my parents for childcare, and then sidled up on our stools.

We drank deep from those salt-rimmed glasses, savoring the slush as it wound down our throats. Our plan was this: hike, eat, drink, repeat. For three days, we stuck close to our plan.

On the first day, we drove to Bandelier National Monument, climbing tall, wooden ladders to peer into the homes of ancient Puebloans. At some point along the hike, we separated—split like atoms in a state now famous for splitting atoms. I ventured deeper into the wilderness and called her name but heard only my echo call back. I searched for signs of human life amid spruce and fir and scrub brush.

Eventually, I rounded a bend, and there she was, peering down at some unknown vegetation.

"Where were you?" I asked.

"Here," she said. "I was always right here."

———

On the drive back to Santa Fe, we attempted to enter the city of Los Alamos. But we couldn't—not without answering various questions at a checkpoint.

Who were we, the guard inquired, *and what was our business in Los Alamos?*

I told him our names. As for our business, I explained that we had none.

"None?" he asked.

"We're just tourists out for a drive."

He demanded our driver's licenses, so we handed them over.

Were we threats to national security? I wondered. *Had our citizenship been revoked?* The guard's eyes fluttered toward Meredith, then back toward me.

"Can you vouch for your passenger?" he asked me.

"My wife?" I asked.

"Your passenger," he repeated.

"Yeah," I said, "I can vouch for my wife."

"Don't go near the lab," he warned, returning our licenses.

He lifted the gate, allowing us safe passage into our country.

———

Back at the hotel bar that night, we sat at a low table draped in shadow. We were exhausted in the best way: our bodies brimming with the electric fuzz of fatigue.

Behind the bar, a TV blared politics and sports. We hadn't the heart for either.

For an hour or so, we tried talking about the beautiful things we'd traveled so far to see. Bandelier's Jemez Mountains. The family of deer. The cave carved like a wound within the rock face. But eventually, we talked past the beautiful things and our conversation returned to gloom.

The truth is, we were so worried about so many people that we forgot to worry about ourselves. This went on for several years.

"To us," we tried, clinking our salt-rimmed glasses in that adobe hotel bar.

The slush cut like knives down our throats.

June 19, 2021
(continued)

On Father's Day eve, Steve, Meredith, the kids, and I visit the public library. A quick trip to return some books—and if we're feeling bullish—pick up a few more.

It is the same library where once, three decades prior, my grandfather—fresh off his knee surgery—hobbled alongside me toward the member services desk so that I might apply for my library card.

"This is a big day," he'd said as we roamed the stacks. "Every book here is now yours."

In the decades between that visit and this one, the library has become unrecognizable. The warmth of those mountain ranges of books has given way to a modern aesthetic in which the books are more hidden than displayed. Though the books haven't disappeared completely, a good number of them have since been withdrawn. As proof, you need only turn to the used-book racks, where for a dollar, you can snag any five you want for keeps.

A few years back, shortly after Meredith's mother died, I returned to the used-book rack to find a dog-eared copy of Elizabeth Enright's *Gone-Away Lake*. In the book's upper-right corner was my former teacher's name—Pflieger. The teacher who, three decades prior, had loaned me this book.

Not just this book, but *this exact copy*.

This copy with her last name in the upper-right corner, and the "withdrawn" stamp from our school.

To hold it again is to be transported to a place I barely remember. To a grade called "Reading Readiness," a pedagogical purgatory for children like me, smushed between kindergarten and first grade.

I wasn't there for academic purposes but for social ones. Because I talked so softly and rarely, an administrator urged my parents to give me a "year's pause" before moving me on to first grade.

My parents agreed. One late-summer day in 1990, I wandered into Ms. Pflieger's room to find a woman who wore her heart all over her body. A woman destined to pour my classmates and me thimble-sized cups of seltzer when our stomachs were rumbly, and who would read to us the soothing tales of a rheumatic rabbit named Uncle Wiggly. Upon noticing my burgeoning love of literature, and the speed with which my fingers flipped the pages, she recommended a book called *Gone-Away Lake*.

"You'll love it," Ms. Pflieger promised. She was right. The book contained no murder, no mystery, and not much in the way of plot. To read it today is to swaddle oneself in the safe embrace of a childhood friend.

But there are no safe harbors on Father's Day eve, not even on Gone-Away Lake. We bypass the used-book racks and head straight toward the children's section, trailing the kids as they break across the open terrain. Steve makes his way toward the spinning racks, where he selects a handful of romances.

As the children load up with half a dozen books each, Steve takes his place in some space-aged-looking "reading bubble" just below the kids' treetop-styled reading room. He leans forward, his eyes peering toward some distant shore just beyond the shelves.

He holds a worn copy of one romance or another in his hands.

Ten days later, when he's gone, I'll find the book face down on the coffee table, splayed open to his final page.

June 20, 2021

"Say happy Father's Day to Daddy," Meredith tells Millie. Wide awake at 6:00 a.m., our girl offers nothing but babble. The older children hug their grandpa tight. Steve and I attempt a backslapping-hug-handshake.

This is not how we expected Father's Day might go—one father struggling to find his breath while the other drives away from half his family. But it is the best we can manage. The version of events that allows Meredith more time with her dad while the older kids and I embark upon our nonrefundable rental cabin in a forest not far from our home.

I tell myself the trip will do us good. We will pack chips and fruit drinks and cheese sandwiches and refer to them as "provisions." We will hike poorly marked trails and then return to the cabin, safe and sound.

On Broadway Street, morning emerges from a mist. My family and I sit alone in Steve's coffee shop as the ghost cars drift past the window. For the moment, our entire world smells like hazelnut. We'd linger there longer if we could.

Reluctantly, the older kids and I make our way toward the back of the coffee shop. Steve trails us.

We squeeze in one more round of hugs, always wondering: *Is this the last one?*

"Happy Father's Day," I say.

"Happy Father's Day," he says.

A different son-in-law might've said more, but what?

We buckle up and begin the 450-mile drive back to Wisconsin. On the far side of the brewery next door, I notice a mural I've never fully seen. A spasm of swirling colors with stylized writing within: *What Are You Waiting For?*

Final Cancer Treatment Preceded by a Surprise
by Steve Ball
June 21, 2021

Reprinted from the Journal Gazette.

I wasn't looking forward to Friday.

My buddy Wayne and I had gone fishing at Ron Lerch's cottage east of Trine Park. Ron passed away before I got to fish the lake, but I did get to fish it—thanks to Ron's son, Chris, and his grandson, Shane.

Unfortunately for me, I was getting tired of fish or, more importantly, cleaning fish.

Last October, I was diagnosed with stage four small cell lung cancer. After barely making it through Christmas, I started a series of treatments that got me well enough to do spring break with the kids and grandkids in Florida. I also got to do a fishing trip in Cabo San Lucas in May. My daughter Meredith's kids came in June for camping at Camp Potawatomi.

Each time I got through one of these "end-of-life goals," I got a little more done up. But they all worked out nicely. It was worth it.

Friday was my last treatment. They were no longer effective, and there was nothing I was looking forward to. The plan was to go on hospice on Saturday.

I opened the coffee shop—Java Bean Café—which I continued to do all through the treatment. That day, I worked the shop and cleaned the fish when I had spare time. Surprisingly to me, I didn't have much spare time.

Usually by 10 a.m., things are slowing down, but not today. I finally got the fish cleaned and just got the guts to the garbage truck as it came down the alley. Now all I had to do was lie back and get ready for my last treatment at 12:30, but people kept on coming in.

There were handball buddies, old widower people I hadn't seen in years, and people I just saw that morning.

Finally, my friend Jimmy Carroll asked for everyone's attention. Jim thanked them for coming to my surprise party. No one was more surprised than I was. By this time, I was on the couch (I was completely done), and I just lay back and listened. It was wonderful—everyone talking and having a good time. I loved it.

Nearly twenty years ago, just after opening, we found out that Caryl, my wife, had rectal cancer. We got through the diagnosis and were planning for what was coming. We were driving and Caryl turned to me and said, "You know, everyone has been so great—if I die, there are going to be a lot of people at my funeral."

I thought only Caryl would look at a horrible situation and come up with something good.

But then on Friday, I was lying back on the couch enjoying everybody having a good time, and I thought: It can't get any better than this—I get to be a participant at my own wake.

Thank you all.

June 23, 2021

Henry, Ellie, and I turn left off the main road toward the fiberglass graveyard—a vast field where busted fiberglass statues go to die. The statues stretch on for acres: every giant roadside attraction imaginable now half-shattered and splayed in the grass. Cows and rabbits and knights and crocodiles. A fractured elephant herd. A bat. Paul Bunyan. A pair of empty boots.

Silence enshrines this menagerie of the strange. If they were in better condition, these roadside attractions would lend themselves to selfies. But these outcasts, entombed in their rural graveyard, are only photoworthy when broken together.

The time: twilight.

The place: Sparta, Wisconsin. Our home for the next two days.

Henry and Ellie disappear behind a giant bulldog, its fiberglass skull cracked in half. Meanwhile, I marvel at a frog whose mouth yawns wide into a slide. The kids loiter in the graveyard, peering at the broken shards collapsed in the knee-high weeds.

Back in Indiana, Meredith and Steve, with Steve's sister, Julie, roam Zion Lutheran—a church that doubles as the site of Steve's former middle school. Meredith is unsure what they are doing there, only that her father has decided he wanted to go. And so, they got in the car and drove to the place where none of them had been in years.

That night, once the kids and I return to the rental cabin, Meredith calls to share with me about their unplanned trip to Zion

Lutheran. A place where, back in 1964, fourteen-year-old Steve and his teammates dribbled a basketball to the sectional finals.

Steve has never been one for sentimentality. That he was determined to visit this place, to take a lap around the pews, reaffirms, in my mind, that he has a new understanding of timelines.

Silence hangs heavy on our phone call as I imagine the juxtaposition.

How just an hour prior, Steve had sat alongside his sister in the pews while the kids and I had peered inside the mouth of a fiberglass frog.

Interview #6
Winter 2022

B.J.: Can you tell me more about that day at Zion Lutheran?

Meredith: He was kind of in a weird place by that point. He was not talking about much. Just kind of walking around and looking at stuff. I don't know. I was also worried that he was going to fall at some point, so I would just kind of follow him around to different places . . . We just drove around. Their [childhood] house had burned down at some point, so we just passed the lot. It's kind of funny. We didn't even live that far from where he grew up, but I never went over to that area of town. So he just kind of showed us around. He wasn't very nice to the priest. My aunt was like, "You know, he's very ill," kind of trying to apologize for him. [*Laughs.*] He just sat there.

June 24, 2021

Because we are in a town called Sparta, I settle in with a copy of *The Iliad*. Seated on the cabin's porch, I glance up from its pages to watch the storm clouds close in like the Achaeans.

This has been the day we've been desperate for—a day of canoeing, swimming, and pudgy pies roasted over the open flames. A day of finding the waterfall. Of pine cones. Of swing sets and hot hikes and chitchat with strangers about all the forgettable things we will never long to return to fifty years later. Or even ten years later. What is memory, really, but a manufactured moment after the fact?

On this day, we drink draft root beer by the gallon. And we opt for the second bag of chips. We rescue lost toys on the shores of a lake. Search for brook trout the length of Ellie's arm.

Throughout the day—when cell service allows—I check in with Meredith.

"What's happening?" I ask as the kids splash in the shallows.

"Well, he was supposed to be cleaning fish," she whispers, "but we found him plugging in the power saw."

"Wait . . . why?"

"I don't know why," she says. "He doesn't know either."

"Was he trying to clean the fish with the power saw?"

"No."

"Was he trying to cut something?"

"Nothing in particular," she says.

Equally perplexing: the round of espresso shots he made for no one.

Odder still: the various papers he burned in the trash can alongside the garage.

"Hold up. He was burning papers?"

"Yes."

"What papers?"

"I don't know," she says. "I don't think he knows. I can't explain it. He's just . . . doing things. He's going to hurt himself."

The worst, Meredith says, is when he wakes up at 3:00 a.m. Those hours when he's mostly roaming the house alone. Or the coffee shop. Or the garden. All those unaccounted hours in the middle of the night.

"There's no telling what he might do," she says.

"God," I try. "You must be so tired."

In the background, Millie wails.

"Gotta go . . ."

"Okay, well call me if—"

"Yeah."

Inside the cabin, the kids play Go Fish while my eyes flitter toward the approaching clouds. I place *The Iliad* face down on the table, then stare, astonished, as the storm unravels a dark ribbon across the sky.

"You guys got to see this," I shout to the kids, engrossed in their game.

They glance up, nod, and assure me it's "pretty cool."

"It's not," I say. "This is a serious storm!"

"Yeah, Dad," Henry says. "We know."

Ahead of me, the raindrops pound atop the lake like tack hammers.

A few feet away, the last gasp of our pudgy pie fire. I try gathering the towels on the porch railing, but already, I am too late.

The night ruptures, the sky splits in two. We are surrounded.

June 25, 2021

Meredith, her sister, and Steve take their seats at an upscale restaurant downtown. The overly friendly waiter approaches to recite the specials. No one at the table has time to hear them; still, they listen. This is the way of things.

"Now then," the waiter asks, "can I start you off with some drinks?"

Steve orders a beer.

The waiter jots it on his pad.

"Are we here celebrating something?" The waiter smiles.

"Nope," Steve says. "I'm just passing away."

"Oh," the waiter says. "Oh. Well, I'm very sorry."

"Thank you."

In the stillness of the coffee shop, I open my laptop. I get to work on the only work my body knows to do. I rub the words against one another, in search of an economy of language that might capture the full measure of a life.

Steven C. Ball, owner of the Java Bean Café and a lifelong resident of Fort Wayne, IN, died on _____ at the age of 71.

Steve is survived by his three children, Jill Garst (Ryan), Meredith Hollars (B.J.), and Michael Ball; his four grandchildren, Addison Garst and Henry, Eleanor, and Amelia Hollars; his sister, Julie Hecht (John); and his brother, Michael Ball.

Steve was born in Fort Wayne on May 30, 1950. In 1982, he married Caryl Armstrong, who preceded him in death in 2015.

Steve was an avid handball player and fisherman. At the Java Bean Café, he served his loyal customers coffee, camaraderie, and the occasional egg sandwich. Much of his clientele made the Java Bean Café a daily pilgrimage. For coffee drinkers of a certain age, it became a social club of sorts: a place to swap stories, play a hand of cards, or provide commentary on the news of the day. Some affectionately dubbed it "The Old Codgers Club." Steve's friend Jim said it best: "We returned not so much for the coffee, but for the connection, thanks to our friend Steve Ball."

To honor Steve's love of fishing, a memorial bench will be placed along the shores of Lake James in Pokagon State Park. All fishermen and women are encouraged to have a seat, enjoy the view that Steve so loved, and take a moment to untangle the line.

A memorial ceremony is scheduled for _____ at _____.

I save the file "Obit.docx." I attach it to an email to my wife.

I write: "Here's a draft of the obit you can tinker with as a family when you're ready. This is just the bare-bones version."

Because I cannot cure cancer, I write an obituary.

When I write "tinker with as a family," I wonder who, precisely, I have in mind.

June 28, 2021

An hour or so before the hospice nurse returns, I offer Steve assistance. He's standing alone, a few feet between the bed and the bathroom. He is stone-faced, his left hand balanced lightly atop his desk. The older kids and I returned to Fort Wayne the previous day to find a man who'd stopped talking. Though silent, Steve remains fully conscious of the world.

"Hey, Steve," I say, "can I help you back to bed?"

He wears athletic shorts and a solid-colored T-shirt. His feet, suddenly swollen, have lost their shape.

"Maybe I can help you back to bed?" I try.

No response.

"How about I help you back to bed."

I place my right hand into his right hand, then cup his hip with my left. I prepare to move us, though I wait for him to move first.

A minute passes. Then four. We stand together, teetering.

Cupping his hip, I recall the time he insisted I join him for a game of handball.

Handball? I'd thought. *Who plays handball?*

Steve did. And maybe half a dozen others throughout the city. At least two of Steve's handball compatriots had suffered fatal heart attacks while on the court. Maybe that's why he insisted I play. At twenty-one, I was not at risk for a heart attack. Merely a good ass-kicking, which was what I had in store.

Stepping onto the court, I'd told myself I'd let him win a few points. No such niceties were necessary. He destroyed me so thoroughly that I wondered if he was even having fun. Though, I suppose dominating your daughter's boyfriend in spectacular fashion is always a little fun.

We continued our "fellowship" in the YMCA sauna, where Steve and I were joined by his band of buddies—men in their fifties, who had more hair across their bodies than a herd of highland cattle. Each of the men looked pulled from central casting from a mob movie: their tufts of chest fur all but swallowing their gold chains. As I tried to regain feeling in my throbbing palms, they trash-talked me to smithereens.

"A win for the old guys," chuckled one man, slapping my back so hard it left a mark.

Sixteen years later, I cup Steve's hip in my hand. Together, we walk nowhere.

Meredith enters the room to find us in our strange embrace.

"Dad," she says. "Where are you trying to go?"

Steve directs his eyes toward the bed.

"Okay, then you have to keep moving," she says.

"Just let me know how I can help you," I say.

But he can't tell me. That's the whole problem.

"Dad, if you don't start walking, B.J. will carry you."

"Mmm mmm," he says, something like terror in his eyes. Sixteen years since our first fellowship. Since the day on the court when my hands were turned to meat.

Slowly, Steve's feet shuffle toward the bed. An eternity passes and then some. He lays down. We lay him down. Then Meredith leaves the room.

This is the last time Steve and I are alone together, though I'm not sure he knows that I'm there. I stand at the bedside, attentive to whatever comes next. Nothing comes next. Not yet.

In the corner beside his closet: a pile of sweat-encrusted handball gloves.

June 28, 2021
(continued)

Following a lunch of cold sandwiches at Steve's house, Meredith turns to me and says, "I think today is the day."

Did she observe something? Intuit something? I'll never know how she knew. Even if I asked, I don't think she could explain it. I don't think I'm ready to know anyway.

The house is as dark as a theater. The curtains, once opened, are now drawn. A few stray beams of light waver toward the oranges to the left of the kitchen sink. The traffic hums down Broadway. The newspaper lies dormant in its sheath.

The air conditioner window unit chills the room. It's too cold for some of Steve's visitors, all of whom have left by now. A few weeks back, when Steve was stronger, Meredith and I had watched him install the upstairs window unit so we could sleep at a more comfortable temperature. We watched the way he knelt alongside the upstairs window, balanced the unit in one hand and a screwdriver in the other. How he stretched the accordion-like side panels of the unit until it fit perfectly. Meredith had begged him to let us help him, but he'd refused. This is how he'd always done it, so he did it again.

When Meredith breaks the news, I'm still holding half a cold sandwich.

"What do you want me to do?" I ask her.

"Why don't you take them to Fox Island?" Meredith suggests.

I am grateful for a task that I can complete, for guidance that will hopefully help everyone or someone at least.

"Kids," I call, "swimsuits on. We're off to Fox Island."

Henry and Ellie peer up from the glow of their grandfather's television.

"Where?" Henry asks.

"A park," I say. "It doesn't matter."

Twenty-six years prior, on the last day of summer, my mother, brother, and I unfurled our towels and laid them along the sandy shores of that beach. A county park just a couple of miles from our home. I was eleven, my brother seven. That afternoon, he and I swam to the buoy and back. We plunged deep into those dark waters, bursting to the surface and then back to shore to sip orange sodas from cans. At day's end, to impress my brother, I poured the final sip of that soda atop my head. I can't explain it. A baptism by soda for the last gasp of summer, I suppose. Followed by my brother's laughter catching in his throat.

Twenty minutes later, upon our arrival at Fox Island, the tinged memory of orange aluminum washes across my tongue. I stare out at the same trees I saw all those years before. The same sand. The same water or close.

"Last one in the lake's a rotten . . ."

Henry and Ellie sprint toward the water, refusing to be a rotten anything.

I have been to this park perhaps a hundred times in my life. To build a birdhouse alongside my dad. To examine owl pellets with my brother. To crack geodes. To net tadpoles. To cross-country ski. To bird. To walk the haunted Halloween trail while pressed tight to my mother's arm. But this moment, I know, will overwrite those memories.

We swim until we can't stand the cold any longer, then towel off and walk counterclockwise along the water's edge.

"Come on," I tell Henry and Ellie, "I want to show you something."

I have nothing to show them, but they believe me when I tell them there's something special just around the bend. We all want to believe in surprises, and so, they follow without complaint.

The reality is that we are here so that we are not elsewhere. And because there is more life in the flecks of light scattering atop the water than in the hospice bed back at the house. The kids have grown weary of vigils. And I have grown weary of asking them to hold them. The thought of another round of "last goodbyes" is more than we can bear. We who are not sick, and who are not dying. At some point, detaching ourselves from our circumstances is the best way we know to carry on. It is less selfish than self-preservation.

We round one bend and then another. We push through the tall grass and cattails. At every opportunity, we crouch low to study a flower. Or a root. Anything and everything that might pass for something worth knowing.

"Oooh . . . what's this one called?" Ellie asks me, pointing to a plant.

"I don't know."

"How about this one?"

"I don't know that one, either."

"Dad, do you know the names of any of them?" she asks, laughing.

"You know, honey, I really don't know."

All I know is that I must keep them here awhile longer. Take more time with each flower, each root, and look closer. That we must rub dirt between our forefingers and thumbs as if something might be gleaned by our attempt. I have nothing to teach them or tell them. Nothing but this moment to loiter and be alive.

On the far side of the lake, a woman baits her hook, casts her line, and creates a ripple in the water. If Steve were here, he'd be doing the same. How many times had I caught him striking that pose: pole in hand in ankle-deep water, a slow smile blossoming across his face?

"Hey, Dad," Ellie says, "look at those crazy dogs!"

Indeed, we have stumbled upon the "dog beach" section of the waterfront. A couple of owners roam barefoot along the bank as their dogs thunder between shoreline and water. The dogs appear recklessly happy in their pursuit of a tossed ball, flinging sand in all directions with their paws. There is time enough to sniff everything. And enough vegetation to keep the tossed ball hidden for a while.

If dogs can smile, these dogs do. And since we can, we try.

Interview #7
Winter 2022

B.J.: What about Fox Island? Can you think hard about some memories there?

Henry: I thought I saw my friend from camp. It probably wasn't my friend from camp, but it was possible.

Ellie: I liked when you thought you saw a dock far away.

B.J.: I did see a dock far away.

Henry: You made us walk all the way around the lake . . .

Ellie: And all we saw was some broken old dock!

B.J.: Yeah, well, it was a place to walk to.

Ellie: I guess.

[*Pause.*]

B.J.: What about you, Henry? Remember anything else from that afternoon?

Henry: I really didn't want to go.

B.J.: To Fox Island?

[*Henry nods.*]

B.J.: Why?

Henry: I knew something was up, and I didn't want that to be the last thing I ever said to him.

B.J.: What?

Henry: Before we left, when he was awake. I just said, "We're going to Fox Island." It was just sad to say it.

B.J.: Do you feel like he heard you?

Henry: Yeah, he was like, "Okay." That was right before he went to bed. Before he fell asleep.

June 28, 2021
(continued)

No sooner do we reenter Steve's house than I'm asked to leave again; dinner, after all, will not retrieve itself.

I reach for a pad of paper. "So who wants what?" I ask.

Meredith, her brother, her sister, and her aunt relay precisely what they want—their food order so detailed it's comical.

"Mild salsa . . . no, wait . . . maybe medium?"

"Pork . . . no, chicken . . . no, pork!"

"Do they still have guacamole?"

"Oh, and can you also get some chips and salsa from the grocery store next door?"

They are ravenous, and as desperate as I am for some momentary distraction.

"I think I got it," I lie, scribbling down words. I click the pen closed. "Now then, who's coming with me?"

Ellie, who's been holding Boppy's hand since the moment we returned from Fox Island, allows her brother to take hold. Once Henry's hand is secure, she follows me out the door and into the van as we begin the half-mile drive to the taqueria.

Upon our arrival, I order something that vaguely resembles the words that I have scrawled on the pad.

"Now what?" Ellie asks.

"Now, we wait," I say, folding her in close beside me. Together, we stand near the back of the taqueria, while around us, a dozen patrons thoroughly enjoy their meals.

From my first moment with Steve, he'd been offering me chips and salsa from the international grocery store next to the taqueria. On this night, we buy those chips again. And that salsa. And their combined flavors—the salt and the spice—remind me of an evening thirteen years prior when I'd asked Meredith's parents' permission to marry her. Maybe less of an "ask" than letting them in on it. The engagement, as I'd conceived it, involved a rather extensive citywide scavenger hunt, the clues to which would lead us to Steve's coffee shop at midnight.

In the days preceding the engagement, I'd explained to Steve and Caryl that I hoped to borrow a key to the shop. For "engagement purposes," I'd said. They conferred with one another with their eyes. Finally, Steve rose, fished the key from a nearby bowl, and handed it to me.

"Okeydoke," he said, excusing himself to the kitchen for more salsa.

It was the closest to a "blessing" I'd ever received.

"Forty-one?" an employee calls, returning me to the present. "Order forty-one?"

We drive back to the house with our bag of tacos. But before entering, I'm drawn to the coffee shop. Ellie and I peer inside the back door's narrow window. My eyes fall to the place on the floor where I took to one knee.

"Dad?" Ellie says.

"Hmm?" I say.

"What are you doing?"

"Remembering," I say.

"Can you remember later?" she asks.

As we enter through the house, I recite the familiar line:

"Burglars," I call.

The sound of the door, closing.

June 28, 2021
(continued)

Because action is preferred to inaction, Ellie leads me back toward the van.

"Honey, where are we going now?" I ask.

"Zesto's," she says. "He needs a chocolate malt."

Steve, who has barely sipped water all day, likely doesn't. But because Ellie knows it is his favorite treat, immediately following dinner, we drive to the ice cream stand.

I pull into the parking lot. Ellie and I race toward the order window.

The line is longer than we'd like. Ellie shifts her weight between her flip-flopped feet. When the young woman behind the counter finally asks for our order, we don't delay.

"One large chocolate malt," I say. "Please."

Inside the stand, the young woman taps the malt mix into the ice cream. She bustles alongside the other teens, adding ingredients to the metal cup before placing it beneath the mixer. The mixer whirs at full throttle, like a throat clearing, before shuddering back to silence. The young woman reaches for a striped cup, a blue spoon, and a blue straw.

"One large chocolate malt," she says. "Enjoy."

Back in the van, we hit a red light.

"Come on . . . ," Ellie pleads. "Come on . . ."

There are no train tracks in sight; still, I assume a train is coming.

We reenter the house, bypassing the kitchen—where the remnants of tacos lay sprawled across the table—until reaching Steve reclined in his hospice bed.

The family lifts their heads just high enough to see Ellie holding the malt with both hands.

"He wants it," Ellie says.

Meredith reaches for a thin spongelike instrument from which she's offered her father droplets of water all day. She dips it into the blue-and-white-striped cup, then dabs the malt to his lips. She repeats. If Steve tastes it, he offers no indication.

Summoning her grace from a place we adults cannot fathom, Ellie holds tight to his loose grip, tethering him to the earth. In her opposite hand, she rubs her worry stone with her thumb.

In the background, Sam Cooke's "You Send Me" wafts from a speaker. On the table, slices of triangular-cut watermelon are in the bowl. There are other artifacts, too: the half-eaten bag of potato chips, the sugar cream pie, the tacos, and the stack of library books. The unripe tomato, the crumb-lined knife. A lime, quartered, its citrus lingering.

Later, I will remember every detail of the day's fading light, the way it pressed through the windows, casting along the blankets strewn atop my father-in-law's bed. The way it summoned us to our twilight vigil, directing us to our chairs. And the person positioned in the pathway of those beams: Ellie, her hand gripped tight to the hand that could not return it.

By 8:00 p.m., the light is a memory. No one prays for miracles, only an end we can endure.

June 28, 2021
(continued)

Millie sleeps in an upstairs room while Henry and Ellie's eyelids begin to droop. They stave off sleep as best they can, but the battle is already lost. Steve's house is too small for us all, so the kids and I have been returning nightly to my parents' house just a few miles away. Our nightly departures are about more than physical space. We want to get away for a while.

"Do I . . . take them?" I whisper to Meredith. She wears a green skirt and a gray shirt. Her glasses cannot hide her exhaustion.

"Maybe a few more minutes," she says.

Sam Cooke sings. Randy Travis sings. Then Sam Cooke once more from the top.

Darkness fills the room, aside from a nearby lamp. This is the quietest the children have ever been. Staring at the man in the bed, I am reminded of just how much he loved walking. How much he enjoyed watching the world pass slowly beneath his feet. How we were always walking somewhere. Around the block. Down the alley. Across the street to nab a few mulberries from the neighbor's tree.

The minutes pass like seasons, until at last, Meredith signals me with a nod.

I walk up the stairs past Steve's old mattress to retrieve Millie.

"Okay, guys," Meredith says with a sigh as we reassemble, "time to say goodbye to Boppy."

The older kids whisper the words, pressing their small bodies against the larger one in the bed. Millie—newly woken—wails enough for us all. We surround him, burrowing our hands and faces into his arms.

Placing my hand in Steve's hand, I think of him giving me the key to the coffee shop. The time we'd played handball at the Y. And that night every November when we'd select the family Christmas tree from the Boy Scouts in the abandoned parking lot where they set up shop. How those Boy Scouts would wrap the tree in mesh before hefting it to the roof of the van. And how, back at the house, I'd steady the tree as Steve guided its base into its stand. How he'd secure it to the wall with wire. And then, once the real work was done, how he'd retreat to the couch with a bowl full of grapefruit, leaving the rest of us to deal with the ornaments.

"Thank you," I whisper.

The kids and I buckle into the van, beginning the slow drive beyond Broadway toward Taylor Street and back toward my parents' house. Past Zesto's and the taqueria. Past the railroad tracks, which at last are not in use. I feel the familiar bump beneath the wheels, cueing me to take a right toward the house. On the far side of Noll Park, I glance past the leafless trees to see my parents' darkened living room through the window.

Up the gravel drive, then back inside, where we are greeted by my parents' silhouette. They have turned off the living room lights, insisting on candles for Steve. My mother lights the wicks. She hugs the children to dust. My father whispers to me how he hates knowing that he will survive the night while the other grandpa will not. My mother smiles as tears stream down her wrinkled skin.

What a luxury (they say but do not say), to live till morning.

Earlier that day, workers installed a new wooden floor throughout the living room. As such, the children now slide across it in their socks. Someone blasts a Taylor Swift song, and for a moment, things are almost good.

Now fully awake, Millie leads her siblings in a floor-sliding routine. Though Henry and Ellie slide twice as far, Millie's attempts provide twice the comic relief. From my place on the edge of the living room, they all reduce to shadow.

"Hey, Grandpa, watch this!" Henry shouts to my dad as he prepares for his longest slide yet. "Hey, Grandpa!"

"Hey, Grandma," Ellie calls to my mom. "Grandma, watch!"

The songs wind down, as do we. We brush our teeth and fit ourselves into jammies. We tuck each other in tight. And then, once we've all left the living room, my mother blows out the candles.

From my place in the back bedroom, I lose myself in Millie's tumbling breaths. But since I can't sleep, my mind veers to the dogs on the beach at Fox Island. The way they'd whimpered with happiness earlier that afternoon. How their joy was not just theirs but belonged to everyone. How they brought it back to us along with the tossed ball. How they shook the water from their coats as if shedding some skin. And how they smiled, or seemed to smile, in the ways that dogs do.

As my eyelids grow heavy, I recite my prayer and its hopeless addendum:

I hope nobody dies tonight . . .

But this time, I'm not even sure that I mean it. We have all made something as close to peace as we can. We played Sam Cooke and Randy Travis. As we write the last chapter of life, we can't revise forever. We have attended to all the things in need of attending. We have not blinked more than we should. We have entered that dark theater.

A few minutes past 1:00 a.m. I receive the text.

Sometimes you know the news before you even hear it.

Interview #8
Winter 2022

B.J.: That last day, I remember you telling me at lunch that you thought that was kind of it.

Meredith: Yeah . . . [my sister, brother, and I] sat around his bed all day and just kind of talked. Played some music. I don't really remember the last words he said. The previous night we all had dinner together at the coffee shop. We had burgers. And he ate. He never stopped eating or drinking or doing stuff for himself until the last day. . . . The second to last night, somebody stayed back with him, and the rest of us walked to Zesto's. And when I got back with the malt, I put it in the freezer for a while, but at some point, he got up and just drank that whole malt. He said, "That was good." Those were the last words I know he said for sure.

June 29, 2021

At 7:00 a.m., I loom alongside my childhood bed, studying Ellie curled within its ancient sheets. In her palm rests the worry stone we'd acquired a few weeks back at the Dickeyville Grotto. Ellie— who cannot keep track of her glasses—refuses to lose the stone.

Henry's fast asleep in the room next door, but since Ellie's the early riser, I know it's best to stay where I am. At last, she stirs to find me seated on the edge of the bed. Her eyes blink. She rubs away the last of the sleep.

"Hey," I say.

"Hi," she says.

"He died," I say.

"I know."

She scoots my way, wraps her small arms around me, as we both accept the sacrament of silence.

"I'm sorry," I say.

"I'm sorry too," she says.

I turn my attention to the worry stone.

"Can I borrow that?" I ask.

She nods and slips it into my palm.

Together, we rise from the bed and into the morning, holding tight to the bearable weight.

June 29, 2021
(continued)

A few weeks back, Steve turned to his sister and said, "I've only got one goal left. I want to live long enough to see my tomatoes ripen."

Meredith and I had been eating those tomatoes for years. No sooner had I met her than I learned of her father's commitment to foisting food upon us. We'd be watching TV, minding our own business, when Steve would stroll our way to deliver a plate of his garden-grown sliced tomatoes. Or some freshly caught bluegill. Or his second-favorite dessert: ice cream topped with crushed potato chips.

Upon learning of his wish to live long enough to see his tomatoes ripen, I immediately reached for the hose. I spent the last two days of his life becoming a one-person flood, dousing the tomato plants to the point of drowning them. I pressed my hands to the dirt and pulled weeds, while feet away, Meredith and the children sat at Steve's bedside.

I imagine many prayers were sent Steve's way during those final days, but mine were directed elsewhere.

Please, let's get these tomatoes moving.

In the hours before Steve's death, the kids took turns holding his hands. I recused myself as often as I could, slipping outside to roam my father-in-law's tomato cages, crouching low among the leafy vines in search of signs of fruit. I found several, though each tomato remained a sickly green.

A few more days. Just a few more days.
We didn't have that many.

———

The morning after his death, the kids and I drive to Steve's house, swing the door open, and stare at an empty bed. For the first time in a long time, the house is quiet and serene; we wrap ourselves within it.

Ellie bounds up the stairs in search of Meredith, while I turn to learn that Henry is no longer with us. Returning outside, I find him in his grandfather's garden, his back turned toward me as he aims the full blast of that hose directly into those plants.

For forty-eight hours, I'd done what I could to fulfill my father-in-law's wish; now, that work goes on through my son. Reaching for the valve, I turn off the water. Perplexed, Henry traces the hose back to me.

Our hands are just doing things. Our bodies are just doing things. It is not instinct that guides us, but memory.

One foot in front of the other, I walk toward him, place an arm around his shoulder, and watch the hose fall from his fingers.

"Come on," I say.

"Okay," he says.

Together, we walk toward the house.

June 29, 2021
(continued)

Just like that, the coffee shop becomes a crypt. I retreat there midday, bypassing the backyard garden and pulling the weighted door open. The shop's walls display the photos that have hung there for years: Steve's buddy Joe, back from the man's high school football days, and one of Leo, Steve's fishing pal, who always knew the best lakes.

Near the back of the shop, I spot a photo of Steve snapped twenty years before. He's posing on the deck of some boat, proudly displaying his fish. I lean the photo against the wall alongside the others now gone.

Instinctually, I press my hand to the air pump coffee dispenser. Half a cup of lukewarm coffee heaves its way into the mug. Seated at the small square table, I cast my eyes toward the cash register. A photo is taped beneath where the total is displayed: Boppy and the grandchildren on a bench at Pokagon State Park.

On the bookshelf, I see the same books that have long occupied that space: *South Side High School Yearbook, 1968*; *History of Fort Wayne & Allen County*, volumes I and II. A few phonebooks are stacked beside a black-and-white photo of Steve and Meredith dancing at our wedding.

I walk toward the kitchenette to retrieve a rag to wipe the place down. I start with the countertops, then move toward the tables. My children's cookie crumbs are everywhere. We can never quite disappear without a trace.

Any surface that can be wiped, I wipe. Any inch that can be cleaned, I clean. I run the push vacuum over the ripped and fading carpet. I wash the mugs, positioning them mouth down in the rack. I tie up the trash. I toss it into the dumpster.

When I'm done, the shop looks mostly the same. No better, no worse. Somehow, it is impenetrable to outside forces like me.

On the coffee table, I spot the broken-spined romance book that Steve checked out from the library ten days prior. I make a mental note to return it.

{ III }

After

August 8, 2021

We are traveling, always traveling, this time to the shores of Lake Superior.

"Do you guys see this fog?" I ask, pointing toward the harbor.

From her place in the passenger seat, Meredith glances up from her phone.

"Guys," Meredith calls to the children. "Daddy wants you to look out the window at the fog."

"Cool," Ellie says.

"Neat," Henry says.

Immediately, their eyes resettle to their screens. Seated on Meredith's lap, Leo—always the good boy—repositions his muzzle toward the damp blanket of fog.

The last month has been a blur of Popsicles and swimming pools and peewee soccer. Of searching for traction in routines with little success. It has been both the longest and shortest month of my life. How to explain this new understanding of time except to admit that I don't? The sun rises, the sun sets, and the in-between hours vacillate between seconds and centuries.

Duluth, we hope, will reset our clocks. Make each minute less of a mystery. But time, for me, will always remain a mystery—some strange currency with which we barter and beg daily.

If we are not passing time, we are killing it. Or wasting it. Or squandering it. Or watching it flitter away. We are making good use of it or not. It drifts, or it fades, or does not. Sometimes we are on central time, and other times mountain time. Sometimes we are on beach time, or lake time, or vacation time. Or borrowed time. Sometimes our time is simply up.

We drive north on US 53. Past Chetek, Rice Lake, and finally Superior, before crossing the bridge into Duluth—a port city overrun with boardwalks and candy shops. And the city's pièce de résistance: the country's second-oldest lift bridge, groaning skyward along its dual shafts.

The lift bridge seemed a novelty back when seven-month-old Henry joined me to watch the ships pass through. Back then, it seemed a perfect way to spend our predawn morning, marveling at the mechanical miracle. I remember Henry's heft precisely. And the furry mane of his lion onesie. And the way the incessant bell announced the bridge's impending rupture, halting traffic on both ends as the bridge ascended.

Since our previous visit to Duluth, my wife now has no living parents. Leo has taken our former dog's place on the leash. The kids have outgrown their swimsuits, and now, there is a third child, who will soon outgrow hers. But the hotel is the same, the lift bridge is the same, and the lake—whose waves slosh on unabated—remains as predictable as an oil painting.

"I got the towels and sand toys," I call to my family, who, moments after I parked the van in the beach lot, disappeared over the dunes.

The fog remains as thick as wool—irrepressible, but gentle, as it penetrates our skin. Or tries to penetrate our skin. The body refuses it entry, keeping the outside world right where it belongs.

When I arrive at the water's edge, it takes me by surprise. The fog lifts its window as the waves gather and retreat like a failed front line. I slacken my shoulders and half a dozen bags collapse into the cool sand. Leo barks at the gulls. They are not getting away that easily.

I reach for my phone and begin snapping photos, capturing Henry and Ellie's bodies turning to gooseflesh as their chattering teeth bite back the cold. Alongside me, Millie watches from the safety of the shore, uncertain if she, too, ought to brave those icy waters.

"Dad, get in here," Henry calls, neck-deep in the iron-blue waves.

I seize up at the thought. But because we've come all this way, I do. I run toward the water, trembling as its net of waves coats my back, catching in the soft webbing between my fingers and toes.

Returning to shore, Henry retrieves the football that Boppy gave him.

"We can't miss," I warn as he hurls it my way, "or the tide will take it."

Time slows, and this time, I want it to. Slows, but does not reverse. Cannot return us to our first visit to this beach, on a July night in 2012, when Meredith and I sipped cans of iced tea purchased for a dollar each from the nearby gas station. The night, while huddled in the sand, we changed Henry's diaper in the beach grass. The night I learned, upon glancing at my phone, that a beloved friend's mother had died.

Was it that night or a different night that I began to wonder if the time I'd lived outweighed the time I have left? If the pendulum had swung from one to the other without my noticing.

Ahead of me, in the knee-deep water, Henry tosses the ball to Ellie, who misses it spectacularly. The ball drifts farther from shore as Henry makes the play, tackling the waves to retrieve it.

"Mom," Henry calls, "catch!"

The football breaks through the fog and cloud-filled sky, a wobbly spiral soaring toward Meredith's outstretched arms. Leo hangs loose on the leash while Millie watches. I watch too, through the lens of my camera, snapping the photo while the ball seems to pause in midair. This is the moment in which there's no telling just what happens next. That touch-and-go-moment. That fingers-crossed moment. The one where all you do is hold your breath and hope.

August 10, 2021

On our last dawn in Duluth, when Millie wakes, I take her to the boardwalk just as I have for the others. She is our third and final child. Our grand finale. I'll miss these walks when there is no one left to carry.

Millie and I walk to the lighthouse and back. Then, we take a seat on a memorial bench alongside the canal. A memorial bench, I imagine, not unlike Steve's, soon to be built along some shore at Indiana's Pokagon State Park.

Behind us, I spot the miniature lift bridge meant for photo ops. Painted near the top of its arch is the phrase "Lift Your Spirits in Duluth."

We are trying, I thought the previous day as I snapped the children's photo. *Why do you think we are here?*

Millie nestles into my arm as the purpled smear of sun changes shape and shade as it warms the water. Seated on the bench, we turn our attention to the bridge, which lifts and lowers.

Sometime after 7:00 a.m., we hear the bell and watch as the bridge rises yet again. This time, it's not for some frigate or yacht but for what must be the smallest sailboat on all of Lake Superior—a boat whose captain and crew consist of a single man.

I wonder what a man might manage when alone and unencumbered. Does his solitude aboard the ships makes for an easier journey, or a harder one?

A line of cars idle as they wait for the sailboat to pass. Their sailboat, I realize, is my train. The drivers' expressions—for whom this daily diversion has surely become quotidian—reflect their displeasure nonetheless. It's an expression we all know well, the face we make when we feel that our time has been stolen.

I imagine the drivers conferring with their dash clocks, gripping their steering wheels tight, as I do for trains. I suspect those drivers are trying the trick I've tried as well: willing one thing forward while holding time right where it is. But both motion and stagnancy require time.

There is nothing to be done. Sometimes, there is nothing that anyone can do. This sailboat has stopped everything but time—a reality those drivers must simply endure.

Seated on the bench with my daughter, it's hard not to find some humor in the scene—all those people at the mercy of the smallest sailboat on Lake Superior.

A sailboat named *Audacity*.

The Wild Horses of Tybee Island
February 1, 2018

We strike out in search of wild horses along the shores of Tybee
Island. It's early February—too cold for shores—but Meredith and
I have traveled thirteen hundred miles from Wisconsin to Georgia,
and we won't be turned away. We slip on sweatshirts, remove
shoes and socks, and walk past the pigeons toward the boardwalk.
Aside from a fisherman casting off a pier, we are the only ones
there.

We scan the dishwater ocean, then turn our eyes toward the
beach.

"So about those horses . . . ," Meredith says.

"Yeah," I say. "About. Those. Horses . . ."

We'd gotten our intel a few weeks back from an only occasionally reliable source: my brother's former grade school buddy,
whom we'd met at an Indiana bar when he was half a pitcher deep.
He'd explained that he was home for the holidays—we all were—
though he'd recently moved to Georgia.

"We're actually visiting Tybee Island in a couple of weeks," I
said.

"You're gonna love it!" he said. "They got wild horses running
all over that place!"

Meredith and I shared our *He's full of it* look.

"There are two rules about the horses," he continued, "so you
better listen up."

We leaned forward on our barstools.

"Rule number one: under no circumstances can you hunt the
horses."

Meredith snorted.

"And rule number two: you can't eat 'em."

This time we broke into laughs.

"I'm serious," he said, excusing himself to refill the pitcher. "They're like . . . protected."

That morning, we train our eyes toward the shore, but there are no wild horses anywhere.

"They're probably just . . . blending in with their surroundings," I reason.

"Uh huh," Meredith agrees. "Sure."

We are nine years and two children deep into marriage, and in all this time, neither of us has ever expressed any interest in wild horses. Or tame horses. It's possible that the subject of horses came up at some point, but who can really recall? These days, we mostly only talk about the important things: who packs whose lunch, and who picks up whom when, and is it gym day, or music day, or art day, and what does that mean for footwear? Where are our daughter's glasses, our son's homework, and their snacks? Which words are for whose spelling test? Who left whose science project out in the rain?

Suddenly a fisherman calls down to us from the pier. He needs help, he hollers. He's got a big one on the line.

Meredith and I hustle his way, unsure of what we're running toward.

"Here," the fisherman says, thrusting the pole into my hands.

The fisherman reaches for a pair of pliers, then retakes control of the pole. He reels with the full heft of his body, a bowing motion, before pulling forth from the brackish waters a stingray, which he lifts tenderly over the railing. For a moment, the creature billows like a sheet on a clothesline before being guided to the wooden planks. The fisherman looks like a puppeteer controlling his marionette—each tug on the invisible line reflected in the creature itself.

He hands me the pole for a second time as he circles the ray with his pliers.

"Keep an eye on that stinger," the fisherman warns, "or it could mean a trip to the hospital."

The creature quivers. If it feels pain, it offers no indication. All it does is live within the situation that has developed.

Meredith and I share our *How the hell did we get here?* look. But we know: we fell in love, we got married, we had kids, we gave them everything, and then, for seventy-two hours, we retreated to Tybee Island in search of wild horses.

Which we won't find, not ever, because my brother's buddy was confused, thinking, instead, of an island two hours to the south.

The fisherman is right—I should be keeping my eye on the stinger. Instead, I watch Meredith's face tighten as the fisherman attends to the silver hook, tearing it from the creature's mouth. The fisherman kicks at the ray with his boot until it flops off the pier and lands belly down in the water. It is not cruelty, but kind-ness—a reality I'd have never known until I placed my body within range of the stinger.

Meredith and I move toward the railing and watch the stunned animal float atop the surface.

We are rooting for life.

Two friends wander onto my deck an hour past sunset. They have come for a backyard horror film—long promised, but long delayed. But at last, we are together again. We settle into small talk, providing the version of updates on families and friends in which everyone is generally good. Then, we break out the food.

"I've got pizza," I say, swinging open the screen door. "One second."

As I enter the kitchen, Meredith exits toward the deck for a quick hello.

She hasn't seen these two since her dad died, which means some acknowledgment is in order.

"Hey," the first friend says, his voice turning quiet. "How are you holding up?"

"Eh," Meredith says. "All right, I guess."

"Really sorry," the second friend adds. "What a difficult time."

Platitudes, even offered sincerely, are still platitudes. Accepting them is not the hard part; it's figuring out how to respond.

I return to the deck with a plateful of pizza and a handful of paper plates.

"Hope you're hungry!"

"What's playing tonight?" Meredith asks, nodding to the projector and the makeshift screen affixed to the side of the house.

"Oh, just this 1980s slasher film," the first friend says.

"Sounds fun," Meredith says, reaching for a slice of pizza before returning inside.

The screen door squeaks, clapping twice against the wooden frame. When we are sure she's gone, the first friend turns toward me.

"What a summer," he says.

"Tell me about it."

"The last time we were here was in June," he continues.

"I remember," I say. "Meredith had just been given all those flowers, but since we were heading to Indiana the next day, we had to schlep them off on you guys. Made your wives happy, at least."

They chuckle.

"How are *you* holding up?" the second friend asks.

What is the right thing to say? That I am good but not great? That I am keeping my head above water? That I am keeping my head? Losing my mind? Finding my family? Failing my family? Holding steady? Holding my wife's hand in the dark?

"Eh," I say, echoing Meredith. "I don't know how to help. Everything I say is the wrong thing."

I wonder if this is true in all relationships. If, regardless of the closeness that's developed, there's no understanding about losing a parent until you've lost a parent. Empathy fails. Commiseration fails. We are all equipped with the same words and phrases, none of which come close.

My friends shift in the lawn furniture. The crows turn loose in the trees.

"Anyway," I say, "shall we get this movie started?"

We reach for plates and pint glasses, returning to the rituals of fellowship.

Over the next ninety minutes, I watch eleven people die and don't care. As the good guys close in on the killer, my eyelids briefly close. I pinch my leg to stay awake to little avail.

Like life, the movie ends with a twist I never see coming and one I don't understand.

"Well," the first friend asks as the credit rolls, "what'd you think?"

"Wild," I say. "Just wild."

August 16, 2021

Upon unloading our gear at the Coon Fork County Park campsite, Meredith discovers what I have forgotten.

"You seriously forgot to pack Millie's shoes?"

"Are we sure she needs shoes?" I ask. "She barely even walks."

This is not the best of all possible answers.

"Seriously." Meredith sighs, collapsing to the picnic table. "How did you forget her shoes?"

"I had other things on my mind."

"Yeah," Meredith says. "Me too."

Six weeks have passed since Steve's death. In sixteen hours, Meredith will wake, wave goodbye, and leave the campground to drive to Indiana for final preparations for her father's celebration of life. She will drive her father's car, which somehow ended up in Wisconsin during one of the many back-and-forth trips. The rest of us will join her two days later.

"I'll figure out the shoes," I say. "Let's just try to have a nice time, okay?"

Shortly after setting up camp, we race toward the lake—all three kids splashing along the rocky shoreline on the edge of our site, where shoes are unnecessary. They slip and fall on the moss but recover. They fill their cheeks with lake water, shooting streams back into the lake from which that water's come.

"Can we try not to swallow it at least?" I beg. They don't hear me; they're too busy being statues in a fountain.

Later that night, I start the fire with ease, thanks to the things I didn't forget—newspaper, kindling, dry wood.

I pull a pack of hot dogs from the cooler while Meredith searches, unsuccessfully, for the roasting fork.

"You remembered to pack it, right?" she asks.

"I mean . . . I think I remembered . . ."

This, too, is not the best of all possible answers.

"First the shoes, then the roasting fork," she says. "What next?"

"The ketchup and mustard!" Henry answers from his place beside the cooler. "He forgot that, too."

"And the bug spray!" Ellie adds.

I reach for Steve's car keys. "I'll be right back," I say.

I drive his car to the dollar store in the nearest town. I park, then notice Steve's Styrofoam coffee cup rolling along the floor mat to my right.

I enter through the store's automatic doors, where a woman in her twenties asks, "Can I help you?"

"Baby shoes?" I ask. "And a hot dog roasting fork? And ketchup? And mustard? And bug spray? And maybe some other things I don't even know I forgot yet."

"Um . . . okay," says the woman. "Well, let's start with the shoes."

In the end, we find everything but the roasting fork—including a few moon-pie peace offerings for the kids.

"Anything else?" the woman asks.

My eyes fall to the assortment of helium balloons floating near the store's front corner.

"And one of those," I say.

"Any one in particular?"

I weigh my options: Happy Birthday, You're a Star, Congratulations . . .

"One I Love You balloon," I say, reaching for my wallet.

Fifteen minutes later, I pull into the campsite to find the rest of the family thoroughly enjoying roasted hot dogs.

"Well, what happened here?" I ask, surprised by their sudden change in mood and self-sufficiency.

"We found a stick," Henry says. "And we stuck the hot dog right on the end of it!"

"You found a stick in a forest, huh?" I smile. "Well, I must say, I'm impressed."

"That's not all we found," Meredith says. She holds up a pair of pink shoes.

"Where did you . . ."

"They were just buried in some bag," she says, waving her hand.

"Shoes," Millie confirms. "Mine!"

Bypassing the children, Meredith walks toward the trunk of her father's car and hugs me.

"I probably owe you an apology," she whispers.

"I probably owe you one, too," I say. "But since they don't make I'm Sorry balloons, you'll have to settle for . . . this!"

I open the trunk to reveal her I Love You balloon. She laughs. "I love it," she says. "I love my I Love You balloon."

"And you'd have never received it had I remembered where I put those shoes," I remind her.

"So thanks, I guess?"

"You're welcome."

That night, as the kids toss pine cones into the fire, I turn toward Meredith and say, "Why don't you take the kayak for a spin?"

She eyes the lake. "Well, I guess I could."

"You should."

She descends the hill toward the water. Sliding into the plastic seat, she reaches for the paddle, then slips from the shore. The kids, Leo, and I—having grown tired of the fire—trail her around the rim of the lake. From our place among the trees, the kids watch their mother's silhouette bob in the dark. It's as if they can't quite understand what they are seeing. She is always there, even at her own expense. Even ten minutes of paddling about in the dark had

to be worth something. The night and the water had to be worth something, as well as the crickets and bullfrogs back on shore.

We cannot be trusted to tell our own stories—I know that now—but I hope there is value in trying. Or forgiveness in trying. Or that trying brings us closer to the truth, at least, rather than farther away.

Ten minutes pass in perfect silence, and the children—who cannot bear silence—interrupt it with impromptu caterwauling.

"Mom!" Ellie calls.

"Moooo-ooommmm!" Henry calls.

"Hey!" Meredith shouts, her voice carrying across the water. "Shouldn't you all be sleeping?"

"No!" shout the older two.

"Shoes!" shouts Millie.

Later, after I tuck the children into their sleeping bags, I meet Meredith at the water's edge. I steady the nose of the kayak as she wobbles her way out of it.

"Your turn," Meredith says, handing me the dripping paddle.

"You sure?" I ask. "Even though I forgot like . . . everything?"

"Not everything," she says.

August 20, 2021

August 21, 2021

We arrive at the funeral home a few minutes after 9:00 a.m. Someone lugs the trifold boards of photos to their places on the long white tables. We are early, so the place is empty, except for where it's filled with light.

"Dad," Ellie whispers.

"Yeah, hon?"

"I'm hungry."

"Didn't you eat breakfast?"

"Not really."

In the before-times, Boppy handled breakfast. It's hard to recall the last time we made ourselves food in Fort Wayne.

Ellie and I raid the funeral home fridge but find nothing but condiments.

"I don't know, honey." I sigh. "How do you feel about pickle relish?"

"Not good."

"Let's see if we have any snacks in Millie's diaper bag."

I hand her some scavenged crackers.

"This will have to do for now."

It is no egg sandwich, but we are all learning to live differently.

I position myself near the front door as the more senior guests begin to arrive. They are a ghost parade of well-wishers, both comforting and not. Many are people I haven't thought of in years, some of whom I figured had long since passed themselves. They come with canes and walkers. They hobble and hack into masks. That they have outlived Steve seems in violation of the natural order. A clerical error in need of sorting out.

Next comes the coffee shop faithful, who gather in the main foyer. I intercept them before they turn tail and try to escape. I encourage them to look at the trifold boards, to share a memory or two in the guest book. They agree—anything to occupy the time.

There is no funeral service, just a two-hour window for remembering. One room for the trifold boards, another for the slideshow. Together, Steve's life is summed up succinctly in one hundred or fewer photos. How foolhardy to think we write our own legacies.

By eleven, the guests manage to push past the lumps in their throats; suddenly, everyone's got some story to share. I screen the stories, and when I hear a good one, I turn toward Meredith and say, "You really gotta hear this one."

A guy named John tells me about Zion Lutheran's 1964 basketball team. How Steve and his fellow fourteen-year-olds won sectionals.

"Is that right?" I ask. "I don't think I ever saw him shoot a basketball."

"Well, he did once," John says. "I've got the team photo somewhere."

Months later, nearly a year to the day of Steve's phone call in the middle of my class, Meredith and I receive a letter in the mail. Enclosed is a photo of the 1964 Zion Lutheran basketball team.

I steady myself against the kitchen table, scanning the photo until I see Steve in the front row, far left. A boy just a few years older than Henry. A boy whose wide-mouthed smile and pumped fist says it all.

Had we possessed the photo months before, it might've made the trifold.

Proof of his life before we knew him.

Proof that the story neither starts nor ends where you think.

August 21, 2021
(continued)

Steve's coffee shop regulars have stayed true to their word, tending the vegetables with enough regularity to keep the garden growing throughout the summer. I imagine the old men in their gardening gloves—weeding, watering, and helping themselves to a cucumber or two.

Following Steve's celebration of life, Meredith and Millie take to the front garden, gathering the last of the tomatoes and piling them along the coffee shop's stoop. Millie fills her cheeks with cherry tomatoes, which retain their tangy sweetness even this late into the season.

"Take it easy on the tomatoes, huh, Mil?" I call from the stoop.

Millie grins, a loose stream of tomato juice squirting from between her teeth.

I laugh. She laughs. Some days, all you can do is gobble up all the beauty you can.

In her flower dress, Meredith blends in with her father's garden. The cars continue driving down Broadway, veering around the curve on the cusp of the shop, unaware of the bounty hanging low from the trellis.

Twilight is threatening. Bedtime is just a few blinks away. The fireflies, if they're out there, remain hidden. The June bugs, if they're out there, have long since collapsed in the grass.

The previous night, upon reentering Steve's house and shop for the first time in nearly two months, we were not surprised to find that both were now mausoleums. We disrupted that deep silence: wiping the coffee shop's tables with the ancient rags, then soaking the air pumps from the dispensers in a bath of hot water. These were our preparations for one last gathering in the coffee shop, which we reopened, for an hour or two, directly following the celebration of life.

That afternoon, once all the guests returned home, I found myself standing alone in the cool shadows of Steve's garage. My eyes turned toward the dormant lawn mower languishing beside the chest freezer. While the coffee shop regulars had tended the garden, they had neglected the grass, which had mostly gone to seed. I filled the tank, primed the pump, then yanked hard on the pull cord. The mower hacked and smoked but survived. In the remnants of the August heat, I cut the grass as low as the mower blade goes.

Tonight, as Meredith hums a lullaby for Millie, I enter the coffee shop to find Steve's last harvest piled high atop a freshly wiped table.

Such abundance, even now.

September 10, 2021

We sneak away midmorning, breaking all the rules. There are papers to be graded and classes to be prepped, but we leave it all behind.

I buckle Millie into her seat, leash Leo, and strike out toward the dog park near our home. Leo trembles in anticipation, releasing a joy-filled whimper not unlike those dogs on the beach at Fox Island. Though he summons every ounce of restraint he's got, upon our arrival at the park he loses control—scratching the van door until I release him.

Millie marvels at her good dog's bad behavior, and to encourage it, howls herself as I unbuckle her from her seat. Together, the dog and one-year-old sprint past the mulch to the sand on the river's edge.

They lead the way toward the water, me trailing just a few steps behind.

Since I forgot to bring Leo's spit-slobbered tennis ball, we make do with a stick. Millie reaches for the nearest one and hurls it all of three feet.

Leo rushes toward the stick—a little disappointed, perhaps, by her throw. Still, he repositions himself around it half a dozen times, hamming up his role as a good dog must while buying Millie a few more moments to root him on.

The game continues until Leo dives nose-first into a patch of flowers, shaking loose the pollen like dust. Meanwhile, Millie reaches for a stick half the length of her body and sends it downriver.

"Go, Leo, go!" she cries, pointing toward it. "Stick, stick, stick!"

She squeals in delight as the stick leaves us, traveling toward warmer waters.

It is almost as if I am not even there. As if the two of them have pushed past some veil and ended up here, on the shore of this private wonderland.

I want to join them there, fully, in this place beside the water. But I cannot. There are still papers to grade and classes to prep. There always will be.

I hold my ground alongside them but not with them. Together, the dog and the one-year-old collapse into a nearby field of flowers. My heart breaks, revealing a new heart within.

September 26, 2021

I wake early, slipping outside the motel room toward the shores of Lake Michigan. We are moving, always moving, to keep the moss from growing across our bodies.

This is the final morning of our last trip of the year—a weekend vacation to Door County. I feel miserable. Mainly because our "relaxing getaway" has become anything but. For forty-eight hours, the kids have fought, and their parents have fought, and we are all to blame. But since the children are children, and Meredith lost her dad, privately, I blame myself completely.

A sour mood. A hot temper. These are the things that I've packed.

The fighting began on Friday night as we drove through a downpour somewhere outside Green Bay. The windshield wipers could not wipe fast enough, so we pulled over at an out-of-the-way gas station with a fast-food restaurant attached. Everyone was tired and hungry and wishing we were home. For once, I wanted my intentions to align with my family's. To want what they wanted. To give what they needed. To be present, aware, omniscient—my mind and body together in a single place.

Stepping up to the cash register, I ordered the children the kids' meal deal advertised on the restaurant's front windows. I provided the cashier with every last detail—drink orders, apple versus yogurt, burgers versus nuggets. Then I placed Meredith's order, then my own. Everything was going as planned until the cashier told me the total, which was twice what I'd expected. The kids' meal deal was not honored. The cashier could not explain why.

Sighing, I returned my eyes to the menu and started the order again from the beginning. Frustrations grew; hunger heightened. And then, midway through my second attempt at an order, somehow it all went sideways again. The cashier could not compute the words I was saying. I could not say the words to help him understand. The total was worse than before.

From across the restaurant, Meredith seethed. "Just. Order. Something."

We could have afforded every item on that menu. We could have walked away with a bagful of burgers and been fine. How embarrassing to admit that I got hung up on the principle of the thing. How I wanted that twenty-year-old cashier to honor the kids' meal deal advertised on the window. Because I wanted something to control. In that moment, I needed to sate that desire more than my family's need for food.

Meredith and I repeated our fight in an encore performance the following night. Something about spoiling the children with the double scoop when the single scoop would have done fine. Something about enabling such behavior. Something about their lack of gratitude and her indifference. We have come all this way, we have done all these things, and everyone—it seems—holds it against me.

They would have been content doing nothing, I thought, *and here I am asking them to live.*

That night, I peered at the ruby-red sunset beyond Egg Harbor and imagined my life in a one-bedroom apartment.

My heart hollowed; my body emptied into a husk. Grief, in those days, shrouded everything. Like a funhouse mirror, it made the big things small and the small things big.

Following that second fight, Meredith and I took to the balcony beyond our lakeside motel room. This was not round three but our attempt to understand the first two—to listen carefully to the parts of our stories we weren't hearing. Our talk twisted in circles, our talk led us nowhere fast.

And then, following a beat of silence, she peered out at the water and said, "This reminds me of that town in Costa Rica. The place with the orange groves."

We'd discovered the town in a travel guide in the final days of our six weeks there. This was in 2007, when we were twenty-two and twenty-three. After three years of our long-distance relationship, we'd traveled to Costa Rica to learn what it was like to wake up alongside one another. Also, to teach English as a foreign language, which was our cover story.

We spent our mornings roaming the mountains beyond our rental property, stumbling upon sloths, monkeys, and a pack of free-range domesticated dogs. For most meals, we ate rice and beans, and a pineapple slice for dessert. Most afternoons—once our classes were through—we'd ride the bus to the beach.

Five weeks in, as the trip neared its end, we decided to leave our home base in Manuel Antonio in search of the town with the orange grove referenced in our guide.

The bus dropped us off in the middle of the empty town, so we flagged a taxi to take us to some place where we could stay the night. The driver, in turn, dropped us off at an off-season hotel several miles outside the city. Using the last of our money, we rented a room, then roamed the orange grove, swam in a pool, and wondered how to find our next meal. We liked the oranges, but we hoped we wouldn't have to survive off them.

That night, by way of broken Spanish, we begged the hotel's proprietor to feed us anything. We explained that we didn't have enough money to take a taxi into town, but we would gladly pay him for a meal at the hotel. After many "por favors," he fired up the grill and cooked us burgers. We had the restaurant to ourselves. Had the hotel, more or less, to ourselves. Amid all that quiet, we could just make out a glimmer of the future beyond those groves.

I don't know why our time on the balcony reminded Meredith of that Costa Rican town. Maybe it had to do with the waves. Or the uncertainty of what came next.

"You've got to understand," she says at last. "I haven't even had time to grieve yet. It's like every time I try, you've got a million things to do."

"Fine." I sigh, reaching for my phone. "Let's get it on our calendars."

She is right; I haven't given her much time. But also, the time I have given her, she hasn't taken. Because grief seems ignoble to her, or like weakness. And because (and I'm speculating here) once you begin the difficult work of unpacking it, you realize that the load never lightens. Better to focus on gardening or cleaning the garage—those tasks more easily measurable. Those chores in which your proof of success or failure is undeniable. You see it in the harvest, or you don't. You can fit both cars or you can't.

Grief is both a communal and solitary act. But much of the work happens alone. In one's head and heart and fibers. In a midnight shudder as the highway rumbles like an ocean just a window away. I wish there were some honest guide to grieving, some map worth following that might lead us to a quiet, uninterrupted place. But grief, for me, means writing the guide and making the map, only to learn that the guide and the map don't work for anyone but you.

For years, I have positioned myself as the problem solver: the one who listens to the problem, examines the problem, and resolves it. For an equal number of years, Meredith has told me to stop after the first part: to just listen. But if I care about her, can't I best show it by finding a solution to her problem? Don't we all want to lessen the pain endured by the people we love? Isn't it an act of love to go beyond the listening?

It is not. Not always. Because "fixing problems" is proof that you haven't been listening.

No matter what I say or do, fix or don't fix, hear or don't hear, there will always be a dead father between us. Below us. Surrounding us. We must not speak ill of the dead, but is it also wrong to resent them?

What I want to say is: *Yes, you are grieving your father, but I am grieving the loss of you both. And I know the depth is different, and the realities are different, but losing a person to life—rather than death—can feel equally hard. Harder, in some ways, because you can't help but feel like a living person can be lured back to the way things were.*

But there is no going back. No "way things were" anymore. With every death, the earth loses equilibrium. Because when one spouse's parents are alive and the other's aren't, the balance is upended. One person can call their dad and the other can't—there's nothing equal about that.

We all want to be the person that the people we love might lean upon. But the leaning, too, requires balance. And trust. And relies upon the unspoken agreement that one can support the other for a time, not as some service but as an extension of oneself for the benefit of both. It is the attempt to return to equilibrium, learning how to lean together to redistribute the newly altered weight.

For nearly two years, we have constantly been ten diapers deep. If it is not soccer season, it is football season. If it is not karate practice, it is gymnastics practice. There is always a class to prep, a child to console, and a room in need of cleaning. A dog to walk. A sidewalk to shovel. A garden to plant. A garden to tear up from its roots. A recommendation letter to write. A student in crisis. A friend in crisis. A family member in crisis. Maybe a marriage in crisis too.

It is easier to blame external factors. To take the passive approach of lamenting what the world has done to us rather than what we have done—or failed to do—ourselves. But a peek inward reveals its own raw reality: every day we make choices that lead us further astray.

I know this because I am a "very serious writer" who is always writing some "very serious essay," or some "very serious book," on some subject to be taken "very seriously." Sometimes the words come, other times not. How much do I really want them? How much am I willing to pay? Is there any truth so revelatory that it's worth giving your life to?

Is writing a book an act of love or the opposite of listening?

————

On our final morning in Door County, I drift from the motel room toward the shores of Lake Michigan, a cup of coffee in hand. Nothing fancy, just some Styrofoam cup I'd filled in the breakfast nook next to the emptied pool. Reaching for it, I'd shuddered as my brain connected the dots: the cup in my hand is the same exact brand Steve stocked in his coffee shop. The same cup I saw, just a month before, still rolling across the floor mats of his car. Somehow, nothing brings me closer to Steve than this cup.

My shoulders, which have been tense for months, slacken. My lungs fill with a forest's worth of September air. I take a sip, and a glug of bad coffee burns down my throat. The waves batter the shore like Achaeans.

Up the stairs, I reenter the room to find my family slowly stirring. The TV is on, and Millie's face is pressed just an inch or two from the screen.

I give the children a round of hugs before joining Meredith, once more, on the balcony.

It's easier to describe what happens next rather than try to explain why or how. The mechanics of this, and everything, remain mostly a mystery. As miracles go, this is a modest one. But even modest ones deserve their due.

I turn toward my wife and lift the Styrofoam cup.

"I know," she whispers. "I saw it too."

Interview #9
Winter 2022

B.J.: When you think of last summer, what do you think about?

Meredith: Not a lot of good stuff. It was pretty hard. I remember him calling me about going into hospice. You could tell he was really nervous.

And I remember that he seemed okay when we first got to Fort Wayne in June. He made some food for us. He seemed to be pretty much himself. But as the weeks went on, his brain started not working as well, and that was hard to see. A lot of times, he just pretended he was okay.

Going to the doctor with him was nice because he had just really felt alone the whole time. He liked having me there to ask questions. He never liked talking about himself and I'm sure he never wanted to complain to anyone, so it was not in his nature to be helped at a doctor's office. He got gruff with people. I think it would have been nice for him to have someone with him the whole time.

B.J.: He did chemo by himself, right? Since like November.

Meredith: Yeah, he did it all by himself.

[*Pause.*]

B.J.: Anything else? Maybe a memory from before that last summer?

[*Pause.*]

Meredith: Well . . . it was nice to go to Florida with him. I'm glad we did that. I also liked when I was there for ten days in early December, when you guys were here by yourself. He really wanted to get a Christmas tree, and I have a video of him decorating it. He always had a particular way of doing things, and when I tried to help him, I did it all wrong. I just had to let him do it.

B.J.: He was a hard man to please.

Meredith: He was just so used to doing everything by himself. Like I said, he did not like being helped. But by the end, he needed help.

[*Pause.*]

The last morning when he was actually awake—was it a Sunday?—he wanted to go over to the coffee shop, even though we'd closed it. So I walked over, made him coffee and oatmeal, and he said it was good. My sister didn't want him walking up and down the stairs—she was afraid he would fall and kept telling him no. But I just thought, "You know, I'll just try to keep him from falling." And I figured that if he fell, at least he could fall on top of me. He wouldn't hit a hard sidewalk. We sat on the front porch for a little bit. He walked over and looked at his tomatoes in the garden. He was saying goodbye to everything.

September 28, 2021

In the middle of Henry's football season, I receive a call from my mom.

"I'm tired," she says, "of missing everything."

What she wants, she says, is to miss less.

"How would you feel," she asks, "if we moved a bit closer?"

Meredith and I have been 450 miles away from our family for a decade. We have never known support beyond ourselves. Almost every moment of our lives, we are at work or surrounded by children. The possibility of my parents moving closer seems, to me, a plan worth considering. These were people we could lean upon and people who could lean upon us. Together, in the ways that we are able, we could try to restore a little equilibrium.

"How would you feel about it?" I ask Meredith one night while doing the dishes.

"They'd really move?" she asks, seated at the table where once, we cracked a bottle of emergency wine.

"There's nothing left for them in Fort Wayne," I say. "I guess she saw a picture I posted from Henry's football game. And . . . she just really wanted to be able to go to one. Like just be able to go to one of his games on a random Tuesday night."

I am treading as lightly as possible, laying out facts as neutrally as I can.

"Where would they move exactly? Like to Eau Claire?"

"Well, that's the other thing I wanted to run by you."

We have been trying to move for months. Not because we want to but because our current home continues to shrink as the children continue to grow. A few weeks back, during another day of virtual school, I found Ellie—in search of a bit of quiet—folded into a milk crate in her closet with her school screen.

"What are you doing?" I whispered.

"Shhh," she said. "Trying to learn."

Our move is inevitable, though I've been delaying the possibility for weeks. I don't want to say goodbye to the backyard river birch. Or walking the kids to school. But when Henry's friend's grandparents mentioned that they were downsizing—and would we like to have a look at their home?—I ran out of wrenches to throw in the gears.

We had a look and liked it. We had another look and liked it more. A two-story in a cul-de-sac with a well-loved basketball hoop. A front porch for summer nights, and pine trees out back to block the highway noise just beyond. A fenced and gated garden. A river birch. And best of all: within walking distance of our current home. In leaving, it seemed, we weren't really leaving at all.

In the months to come, I'd wake early and strike out beyond the boundaries of my old neighborhood to familiarize myself with my new one. I wanted to see the way our future house looked before the sun rose. Most mornings, while passing my children's elementary school in the dark, I'd glance toward the flag snapping in the morning wind. I'd cut through the pines behind the school, en route to the walking path along the soccer fields. Then, while the stars were still out, just barely blinking, I'd approach our future home and try to imagine ourselves within it. I'd imagine which window led to which bedroom. I toured the whole place in my head. Then, before Henry's friend's grandparents might peek out the window to catch my staring, I'd return home just as my family rose from their rooms.

We wanted to buy that house; the only uncertainty was who might buy ours.

"My parents said they would," I tell Meredith, turning away from my dishwashing. "They said they'd buy this house, and we could move."

"Really?" she says.

"Really," I say.

"Well," she says, pondering the possibilities, "I think that sounds . . . great."

"Which part?"

"All of it."

The following February, while attempting to box up our belongings, I'll discover one of Ellie's second-grade writing worksheets crumpled in the corner of her room. On it, she'd composed several sentences about our impending move, including: "My house is along the highway," "I've been to my new house," "My family is buying a house."

But then, on the worksheet's last line, her declarative statements veered toward the philosophical.

"Why," she wrote in her earnest scrawl, "does the world move so fast?"

November 24, 2021

A week before we sign the papers to buy a house and sell one, we make the drive—for the second to last time—to Fort Wayne, Indiana. My brother, Brian, and his girlfriend have come home for the holidays, too, one last gasp of togetherness in our home on North Washington Road.

The family home—a 2,300-square-foot, midcentury ranch—was designed by my grandmother in 1955. This place is special: complete with an Anne Frank–inspired spinning bookshelf (my grandparents were Jewish), two-sided cabinetry (they appreciated easy access to dinnerware), and a row of windows along the home's exterior that captured the morning light. Since its construction, no other family has ever lived within its walls.

Because we are meeting Janae for the first time, we all try a little harder. My mother assembles a veggie spread and attempts my grandfather's "world-famous" oyster dip. My dad agrees not to play the same three songs on guitar. As an icebreaker, we play a game involving hitting oneself in the face with a pie. Laughter erupts. Whip cream splatters. The fireplace froths with flame.

As Thanksgiving eve tradition dictates, that night we drive downtown so that Janae can admire the giant Merry Christmas wreath affixed to the city's skyscraper.

I wonder if Henry and Ellie remember the circumstances that led us here the last time: our Christmas Eve search for the Christmas spirit. That night, like most nights, seems so long ago now. It is painful to consider all that has changed—and all that hasn't—in the time between our visits.

Today is the one-year anniversary of Meredith hearing her father say, "Stage four small cell lung cancer."

We are still here.

November 25, 2021

A few years back, Steve informed Meredith and me that he was starting a "podcast"—an astonishing development for a guy who never used a computer.

"What'll it be about?" Meredith asked.

"The coffee shop," he said.

Though his "podcast" never materialized (at least not beyond the memory card on which the recordings were stored), it has one listener, this dark November morning, when I discover the recorder tucked on a shelf in the coffee shop.

I press play, then listen, as the voices return to this space like an echo.

"Now it's recording," says the voice of a coffee shop regular.

"Now it's recording," Steve repeats. "So if that's going, it's recording?"

"Yup," says the coffee shop regular.

"Okay . . . and then I push the pause, or I push the record, if I want it to stop recording?"

"You can push stop to stop, and pause if you just want to pause."

Eventually, the instructions give way to the field recording. Steve places the recorder on the countertop. I listen as some past morning returns to today.

"You should have seen Ron try to go fishing on Monday," Steve said to his coffee shop crowd. "We did real well until we lost that anchor."

"You lost an anchor?" asked a second voice. "That big anchor? How'd that happen?"

"Joe had it tied up real weird. He had a knot and then he had a thing tied around the knot, but he didn't have the two ropes tied together."

The room erupted with laughter.

"Oh Christ, I bet he lost it," said the second voice. "Was it your anchor or his?"

"It was Joe's anchor," Steve assured them.

The room erupted again.

I glean what I can from the recording, but the story is only half there. Something about fishing, then the Amish, then a rental car, then Buffalo, New York. San Antonio. Lake James. Something about a wedding involving a woman named Catherine. Parkinson's disease. World War I. One hundred and twenty dollars. A man who speaks five languages. Cindy's daughter. In the background, I can just make out the din of cups and dishware clattering back to the countertops.

"I think my handball days are coming to an end," a third voice said to the second.

"From what I saw today," said the second voice, "you still look pretty good."

"I'm going to play for as long as I can," said the third voice.

"Push it to the limit," said the second voice. "You'll be better off."

I fast-forward to the next recording on the memory card. Then the next. Eavesdropping.

In total, Steve's got four or so hours of material. None of it is anything of note. But because it is not, I find myself doubly engaged. What he's captured is a time before the conversation mattered. Back when discussing nothing at length seemed a good way to pass the time.

Standing alone in the coffee shop, recorder in hand, I'm hoping for some direct address from Steve. Some secret wisdom sprinkled in amid the banter. Just a hint of the future we've got coming. Or a little guidance on where we go from here.

The recording runs out long before any revelations.

I stop the recording. I replay it once more from the start.

"Now it's recording," says the voice of a coffee shop regular.

"Now it's recording," Steve repeats.

December 26, 2021

Seventy-two hours before leaving my childhood home forever, I cross paths with my ninth-grade English teacher, whom I haven't seen in nearly two decades.

"Mrs. Hancock?" I ask.

It's 5:30 a.m., the day after Christmas. We are both out for our early morning strolls.

She pauses at the sound of my voice—familiar yet forgotten.

"It's B.J.," I say. "B.J. Hollars."

"B.J.?" she says, releasing a slight chuckle. "How are you?"

"I think I owe you an apology," I say. "Last night, while cleaning out my bedroom, I found some papers I wrote for you," I begin.

She laughs.

"I mean, who quotes themselves in an epigraph?" I sigh.

"What brings you back to Fort Wayne?" she asks.

My parents, I explain, though now we are visiting for the last time. Since my wife's parents have passed, and my parents are moving to be with us in Wisconsin, this is our last trip to Indiana.

For three mornings in late December, I continue my predawn walks, which serve as my personal Fort Wayne Farewell Tour. Stops include Lindley Elementary School, the Towpath Trail, and the fringes of Eagle Marsh Nature Preserve. Other highlights are beyond walking distance: my last hike at Fox Island and visiting, for the last time, my grandparents' graves at the cemetery.

But leaving the family home is what I expect to hurt the most. In the days leading up to our leaving, I take out my phone to record the sound of the front door closing, the rumble of the gravel beneath my ambling feet.

But on this morning, I am confronted with a farewell to a teacher I imagined I'd already lost for good. Our predawn strolls determined otherwise. That we are reunited beneath the glow of a red light at the five-way stop between our homes, signals, for me, that the world is capable of reversing course, if only for a moment.

Once, this teacher and I dedicated fifty minutes each afternoon to unpacking metaphors, as we grew up and old in parallel lines. But now, in our last togetherness, we have no time for metaphors.

She fades into one darkness, I into the others. It's as simple, and complicated, as that.

As darkness descends on Fort Wayne, we enter the Java Bean Café. Meredith and I are joined by her brother, who's younger by three years. As we work the key into the lock, it feels as if we are trespassing. In the coming months, once the paperwork's complete, we will be.

We turn on the lights and watch familiar shadows scatter. Though much of the shop's furniture has been sold or junked, the espresso machine remains firmly atop the counter. Moving it would be at least a two-person job; we have nowhere to move it anyway.

I pull open the drawer beneath the cash register and am startled to find a place still untouched. Inside are all the usual, useless things: loose notes, lost keys, a queen of hearts, a six of diamonds. A dollar, a pen, a clipped obituary announcing the death of his beloved buddy Joe. Buried even deeper in the drawer is a mini bottle of some cinnamon-flavored booze.

I hold it up for the others.

"I guess he was saving it for a special occasion," I joke.

We enter the house, which holds more remnants of Steve: a mattress, bed frame, and a playpen filled with pillows and wadded sheets. There's enough left that it would be a pain to clean, though the new owner, a friend of Steve's, has agreed to pitch whatever's left.

We push past the dictionary still on the countertop and retrieve three red plastic cups; into each we pour a third of the mini bottle of booze. Meredith's brother and I grin at the goofiness of it all.

"To Steve Ball!" Meredith toasts.

"To Steve Ball!" we echo. We clink plastic cups like college kids, wincing as the booze burns our throats.

That night, we loiter inside Steve's house. Then, we brave a few blocks through the chilled night, tiptoeing down the slushy streets toward Meredith and her brother's childhood home. When we arrive at the house that is no longer theirs, Meredith and her brother peer at the orange hues emanating from the windows in the rooms that were once theirs. They share a memory of sneaking a few scenes of *A Nightmare on Elm Street* at an astonishingly young age. They chuckle, settling into an unsettling moment from their past.

Then, we retrace the route in reverse, back toward the home where their father died. We turn off the lights and lock the door.

On the drive back to my parents' house, we do not say what by now we all must know.

Everything we do here, we are doing for the last time.

———

On our last morning in my family house, Meredith and I buckle the kids into the van and wave goodbye to my parents. But before I put the van in reverse, sentimentality takes hold.

"I'm sorry," I say, retreating from the van, "I just need to make one last sweep of the house. In case we forgot something."

Bracing myself in the doorway of my emptied childhood room, I put into words what I've failed to previously: that my parents are choosing to leave the place they love in favor of the people they love. They wouldn't have, I realize, were it not for Steve. His death cracked open the last window, showing them a way out.

Down the long hallway—past the bookshelf, and the cabinetry—I make the walk back to the van.

I buckle, I breathe.

"Ready?" Meredith asks.

We take Reckeweg to Illinois Road before driving onto US 69.

For one lingering moment, I gaze into the rearview: securing the city—and its people—to memory.

What Death Is
2023

For Millie, now three, her memories of Boppy are hardly hers at all. They are memories once removed—our shaped story passed on to her. She remembers nothing of the plush cow in Florida, though the plush cow remains. She has no recollection of the stroll they took around the neighborhood Christmas tree in Fort Wayne, though she has the photo as proof. All firsthand experiences have faded; she makes do with the details we give her.

One night following toothbrushing, Meredith shares with Millie how Boppy had a habit of rinsing his mouth straight from the spigot. He'd bow his head beneath the bathroom sink, placing himself at the mercy of that water. The water would catch in his mouth, he'd gargle, then spit. Toothbrushing complete.

Millie has since made it her mission to continue this tradition. Like Steve, she forgoes a rinsing cup, opting, instead, to pull the upper half of her body all the way to the sink, her small legs kicking at the cabinetry, at the air, as she leans her hips into the curve of the countertop. She slurps, spits, then lowers herself to her plastic bathroom stool.

The work complete, she'll turn toward her bedtime preparation companion—either Meredith or me—and proudly announce, "That's how Boppy do it!"

The same strange ritual, night after night after night.

———

A few months back, while seated alongside me on the couch in the dark, my droopy-eyed girl curled into the fold beneath my arm. Shortly before sleep, she lifted her heavy head toward mine and said, "Dad?"

"Hmmm?"

"What death is?"

The question was not a curveball but part of an ongoing conversation on how people, and animals, and all living things, at some point disappear.

"It means gone for good," I told her. "It means no longer being alive."

"Like Boppy," she informed me.

"Like Boppy," I agreed.

She pondered this for a pause as long as a dash.

"Maybe he died because . . . because . . . ," she began.

"Because why?"

"Because . . . maybe because . . ." She yawned. "Because . . . sharks."

Sleep took her before I could question her further. It seemed as good an answer as anything else.

———

A few months back, while driving home from the grocery store, I noticed Millie being suspiciously quiet in her car seat.

"What are you thinking about?" I asked her.

"I don't want to tell you," she said.

"Oh, come on!" I laughed. "Now I really want to know."

"Just . . . beautiful things," she said.

"Beautiful things like what?"

"I'm not telling you!"

A different parent might have let the matter drop.

"Millie, I have to know."

"No!"

"Millie!"

"I'm not . . . telling!"

Five minutes passed. We parked the van in the drive.

"Snails," she revealed as I unbuckled her from her seat. "There. Finally, are you happy?"

December 29, 2021

An hour after we wave farewell to Fort Wayne, we pull off the highway toward Pokagon State Park. We pay the out-of-state entrance fee, then begin roaming the wilderness in search of Steve's memorial bench.

"Is it this way?" Meredith asks, pointing toward a snow-packed trail.

"I don't think so," I say, unfolding a slip of paper from my pocket. "If I'm reading this map correctly . . ."

We're in trouble, I realize, *if we are at the mercy of my map reading.*

Even in ice-encrusted winter, returning to this place transports me to the more carefree days of summer. Those three days each August when Steve lugged his tackle to the lake while the rest of us lounged beachside. Three days building sandcastles with the kids and swimming to the buoy and back. In the mornings, Steve often retreated to his rental rowboat, returning midday with a cooler full of glassy-eyed bluegill and perch. But some days, he'd forgo the boat in favor of a lakeside bench.

So far, all efforts to find Steve's bench have been thwarted. Our casual stroll through the woods has deteriorated to something closer to a forced march, which the children and dog want no part in.

An hour earlier, we'd come so close. Along the frozen beach, the kids and I had wiped the snow from a bench's memorial plaque to see the name Steve Baldridge.

Steve Baldridge?

Was this some terrible typo or just another Steve?

The park rangers assured us it was the latter, and that to find our Steve—Steve Ball—we needed to park on the edge of the closed road on the opposite side of the park. Which we did, continuing our journey on foot.

"Are we almost there?" Henry moans.

"Please say yes," begs Ellie.

Meredith, who holds Leo's leash in one hand and Millie's hand in the other, sighs. We are too cold and too tired to continue—the warmth of the minivan beckons.

"Can we just go?" Meredith asks at last, freeing herself from Leo's leash.

"I'm just going to run ahead really quick," I say.

She gives me her *I wish you wouldn't* look.

"Super fast," I promise.

Why am I so desperate to find the bench?

Because over the past thirty-six hours, my wife and I signed our wills, waved goodbye to our childhood homes, and left the city where we'd grown up. In three months, my parents will leave too. Meaning we have no plans—or reasons—to ever return to this place. Except perhaps to return for this bench, assuming I can confirm that it's there.

Ahead of me, on a slight promontory jutting toward the blue-gray water, I spot a snow-covered bench.

This is it, I think. But that is not it.

I bypass several more benches until arriving at Steve's—the last on the rim of the water. The bench is neither better nor worse than I imagined. It is precisely a bench in the ways that benches are. I do not sit. I do not rest. Instead, I wipe the snow from the center of the uppermost plank, revealing a message that reflects exactly what I'd scrawled on the order form:

In Loving Memory of Steven C. Ball, 1950–2021
A Perfect Place to Untangle the Line

I steady myself against Steve's bench and peer out at the water. Fourteen months prior, I'd done much the same thing: pressed my hand against a cinder block wall outside a lecture hall.

For a full minute, I stand alone in those weeping woods as thick dollops of snow slide off the fanned branches. Beneath me, the soggy earth creeps into boot liners.

Meredith should be here, I realize.

Suddenly I can't get back to my family fast enough. Sprinting through the snow, I track my boot prints back toward the van. Past the vestiges of last summer—a frosted leaf pile, an ashen fire pit— until I hear voices rippling across the winter air. Eventually, I spot my wife leaning listlessly in the snow light just beyond the van.

"Hey," I gasp. "I found it!"

"Seriously?" Meredith asks, straightening. "How is it?"

"Great," I say. "It's one great bench."

I show her the photos I snapped, and she agrees.

"Can we please go now?" Ellie calls from the back seat.

"Just give us a sec," I say.

The morning is quiet and windless; stillness settles in the pockets of piney air. I am waiting for some acknowledgment from the universe that we are okay.

The universe offers nothing; nature sheds neither tear nor leaf. Indifference is its own kind of god.

Meredith and I buckle the children and then ourselves. The road is long, at least.

March 13, 2022

My parents move to Wisconsin on a Sunday in March, the sun, miraculously, shining. We have been stuck in winter's thrall for so long that anything other than snow and sleet has become somewhat hypothetical. But at last, we have outlasted it. Credit the dewy rain that thawed the last vestiges of ice. Difficult as they can be to endure, the beauty of the seasons is that they always inevitably change.

My family and I await their arrival in our former home's sun-dappled drive. The home that was once ours is now theirs. The stitching of worlds is complete.

I watch as their two-car caravan pulls into view. My mind turns to fuzz as I try to make sense of it: what was once abstract has turned tangible. My parents are suddenly here. And not for a day or a week or a month or a year but for the duration of their lives. We will dispense with phone calls and video chats. Now, we'll just knock on their door.

Ellie and Millie pause mid puddle jump to run gleefully toward their grandma. Their felicity splits from the seams.

"We made it!" my mom cries, lowering herself to the sidewalk as the girls engulf her, their bodies pulled close. For a moment, Henry hangs back, standing shyly beside Meredith before unfolding his arms to embrace his remaining grandpa.

"Henry," my dad says, laughing. "You're getting so big! Must be all that football!"

From the front porch of our former home, Meredith and I watch the scene unfold. I turn toward her, and she surrenders a smile.

"Well," I say, "I guess this is happening."

"Good," she says. "I'm glad."

The afternoon turns luminous. The sun streams through the trees that once the crows called home. My mother rises and walks my way, unencumbered by time.

I do not perform the grown-up son shamble. This time, I stride toward her.

"Hi, Beejie," she says, standing on her tiptoes to hug me.

"Hey, Mom," I say, "thanks for coming."

August 2022

Days thrum by until the months become a year and then some. In the backyard of our new home, the vestiges of the garden rot in the land where they grew. The cucumbers turn white with fungus. The squashes collapse into themselves. Another season fades toward twilight as I close the garden gate.

Returning to the deck, I spot flies gathering around a pile of loose-skinned cherry tomatoes. I don't think, I just fill my fists with tomatoes, then walk them toward the edge of the yard. I toss them past the barbed wire fence into the no-man's-land between the highway and our home.

It seems innocuous enough—a little light yard work, nothing more.

Only later, when Meredith returns to the deck to find them missing, do I realize what I have done.

"You just . . . tossed them?" she asks.

"I'm sorry," I say. "I had no idea."

The previous summer, we'd saved seeds from Steve's last harvest and planted them in our garden. Most of them never took root, but some of them did. They became a delicacy far too precious to eat. We saved them, hopeful that those second-generation tomatoes might preserve the lineage into the following year.

They are just tomatoes, but also not. I think back to the cancer survivor at my summer camp who once told me, and all his bunkmates, that "sometimes the cancer leaves, but the ghosts don't."

Sometimes ghosts look a lot like tomatoes. Other times, a bit like coffee beans.

For Steve, it was the latter that most sustained him. Because coffee beans meant fresh coffee, and fresh coffee meant he always had a crowd. Steve loved a good crowd. Loved the way his patrons strolled through his door as if they owned the place too. It was not his, but theirs, proof of which he witnessed daily when the parade of regulars helped themselves to a cup from the air pump coffee dispensers. Steve loved how his patrons gave him a hard time when the coffee ran dry, and he also loved returning fire. If you couldn't take it, you didn't dish it out. And everyone dished it out.

For Meredith, the tomatoes were what mattered. Because her father had tended to them. Planted them, watered them, and shared every one that clung to the vine. How many July afternoons had her father handed her a bowl of sliced tomatoes? How many times had he offered me the same?

Meredith returns to the kitchen to slice a watermelon, while I retrieve a stepladder from the garage. I steady it beside the wooden fence post, whose circumference is no more than six inches. The barbed wire wrapped around the post has been there nearly as long as the highway. Rust coats the spikes, daring me to breach the line. I position my fingers on the wire. I climb three steps to the top of the stepladder. At the proper height, I place my left foot atop the fence pole, balancing on one leg like some karate kid mid crane kick. I push off, propel upward and over, into the no-man's-land. I am surrounded by pockets of quack grass nestled within the knee-deep thistle. Together, they make for a soft landing. A few hundred feet away, the rushing highway blurs. Everyone is going someplace in a hurry. I peer back at our home, which from this distance resembles a two-dimensional plane. In the foreground, an empty hammock rocks alongside the river birch. The last of the petunias wither in their terra-cotta pots.

Inside the house, Meredith continues slicing the watermelon.

Maybe she feeds a stray piece to the dog. Or the baby, who is no longer a baby anymore. Maybe she peers out the kitchen window and sees me staring back, separated by a barbed wire fence that I have safely crossed once, but only once.

Months later, the children will confirm that this is true: that she had watched me, that they all had. They'd stood in a line before the sliding glass door and wondered how hurt I might get. The kids will tell me how they all felt a little helpless just watching me there, which is how I'd felt all along.

In another version of events, I do not make it back the way I've come. In that version, I am stuck on the far side of the fence for hours. Trapped within view of the place I cannot quite return to. Maybe I walk down to the highway and hitch a ride back to the neighborhood. Maybe I just keep walking.

Regardless, first I have tomatoes to find. Kneeling, I reach toward the earth.

Interview #10
Winter 2022

B.J.: Anything else you want to say?

Meredith: Oh, I don't know.

[*Pause.*]

When we went for walks when I was a kid, he'd always say, "Do you know what time it is?" and I'd say, "It's turn time!" Then he'd hold both my hands and spin me around. He was just a good dad. I guess that's pretty much it.

OBITUARY

Steven C. Ball, 71, a lifelong resident of Fort Wayne, IN, died Tuesday, June 29, 2021. He was owner of the Java Bean Café. Steve was born in Fort Wayne to Ellen and Adolphus Ball. In 1982, he married Caryl Armstrong, who preceded him in death in 2015. Steve graduated from IPFW with a degree in chemistry and spent most of his professional career working in chemical waste management. This work took him to Indonesia, Hong Kong, and Thailand, the latter being a place he loved and traveled back to often. In his free time, Steve was an avid handball player, gardener, bike rider, and fisherman. In the last 20 years of his life, Steve found a second family after opening the Java Bean Café, on Broadway Street. At the Java Bean, he served his loyal customers coffee, camaraderie, and the occasional egg sandwich. Steve's shop became a daily pilgrimage for much of its clientele. For coffee drinkers of a certain age, it served as a social club: a place to swap stories, play a hand of cards, or provide commentary on the news of the day.

To honor Steve's love of fishing, a memorial bench will be placed along the shores of Lake James in Pokagon State Park. All fishermen and women are encouraged to have a seat, enjoy the view that Steve so loved, and take a moment to untangle the line. Please join us for calling hours (and coffee!) from 10:00 a.m. to noon on Saturday, Aug. 21, 2021, at Midwest Funeral Home.

ACKNOWLEDGMENTS

Writing, like grief, is a lonely business. But less so when surrounded by so much love.

Thank you to my inspiring students at the University of Wisconsin–Eau Claire, who help me through the hard days. To my colleagues and friends at the University of Wisconsin–Eau Claire: Chancellor Jim Schmidt, Provost Patricia Kleine, Executive Director Kimera Way, Interim President Julia Diggins, Dean Aleks Sternfeld-Dunn, Dean Carmen Manning, Chair Jan Stirm, Jon Loomis, Allyson Loomis, Molly Patterson, Brett Beach, Dorothy Chan, Asha Sen, Sarita Mizin, Kaia Simon, Jonathan Rylander, David Jones, David Shih, Bob Nowlan, José Alvergue, Stephanie Farrar, Stephanie Turner, Theresa Kemp, Joel Pace, Cathy Rex, Matt Seymour, Stacy Thompson, Blake Westerlund, Lynsey Wolter, Frank Fucile, Heather Fielding, Amy Fleury, Shelley Donnelly, Sara Monahan, Liz Kitzmann, Nick Butler, John Hildebrand, Max Garland, Bruce Taylor, Patti See, Greg Kocken, Justin Patchin, Jason Spraitz, Paul Thomas, Jeff DeGrave, Joanne Erickson, Candis Sessions, and Alaina Guns (and so many more).

Thanks to Erica Benson and the Office of Research and Sponsored Programs at the University of Wisconsin–Eau Claire, whose support proved vital to this project. Thanks, too, for the support provided by the University of Wisconsin–Eau Claire Academic Affairs Professional Development Program.

Thank you to the Wait! What? Writers, especially Eric Rasmussen, Ken Szymanski, Julian Emerson, and Andy Patrie, all of whom shine lights down the darkest roads.

To Maggie Pahos—who understands the arc of feeling. To Dale Easley—who feels the arc of it all. To Brendan Todt—who keeps pushing the parallel lines toward infinity. To the Dayton family for providing the good kind of plenty.

To Mom, Dad, Brian, and Janae—for babysitting and bearing witness.

To Jill, Ryan, and Addie Garst, and Michael Ball, all of whom grieved and lived alongside us.

And finally, to Meredith, Henry, Ellie, and Millie—together, we endured.

B.J. Hollars is the author or editor of more than a dozen books, most recently *Wisconsin for Kennedy: The Primary That Launched a President and Changed the Course of History, Go West Young Man: A Father and Son Rediscover America on the Oregon Trail,* and *Midwestern Strange: Hunting Monsters, Martians and the Weird in Flyover Country.* His nonfiction has garnered awards, including the Truman Capote Award for Literary Nonfiction, the James B. McMillan Prize in Southern History for Culture, the Council for Wisconsin Writers' Blei/Derleth Book-Length Non-Fiction Award, among others. His work has been featured in the *Washington Post, Parents* magazine, NPR, and elsewhere. He is a professor at the University of Wisconsin–Eau Claire, where he directs the Chippewa Valley Writers Guild and is the founder of the Midwest Artist Academy.